Regional Security and Anti-Tactical Ballistic Missiles: Political and Technical Issues

William A. Davis, Jr.

Special Report
1986

A Publication of the
INSTITUTE FOR FOREIGN POLICY ANALYSIS, INC.
Cambridge, Massachusetts, and Washington, D.C.

PERGAMON • BRASSEY'S
International Defense Publishers

Washington New York Oxford Toronto Sydney Frankfurt

Pergamon Press Offices:

U.S.A. (Editorial)	Pergamon-Brassey's International Defense Publishers, 1340 Old Chain Bridge Road, McLean, Virginia 22101
(Orders & Inquiries)	Pergamon Press, Maxwell House, Fairview Park, Elmsford, New York 10523, U.S.A.
U.K. (Editorial)	Brassey's Defence Publishers, 24 Gray's Inn Road, London WC1X 8HR
(Orders & Enquiries)	Brassey's Defence Publishers, Headington Hill Hall, Oxford OX3 0BW, England
PEOPLE'S REPUBLIC OF CHINA	Pergamon Press, Qianmen Hotel, Beijing, People's Republic of China
FEDERAL REPUBLIC OF GERMANY	Pergamon Press, Hammerweg 6, D-6242 Kronberg, Federal Republic of Germany
BRAZIL	Pergamon Editora, Rua Eça de Queiros, 346, CEP 04011, São Paulo, Brazil
AUSTRALIA	Pergamon Press (Aust.) Pty., P.O. Box 544, Potts Point, NSW 2011, Australia
JAPAN	Pergamon Press, 8th Floor, Matsuoka Central Building, 1-7-1 Nishishinjuku, Shinjuku-ku, Tokyo 160, Japan
CANADA	Pergamon Press Canada, Suite 104, 150 Consumers Road, Willowdale, Ontario M2J 1P9, Canada

Library of Congress Cataloging-in-Publication Data

Davis, William A., 1927–
    Regional security and anti-tactical ballistic missiles.

    (Special report/Institute for Foreign Policy Analysis)
    Bibliography: p.
    1. Europe—Defenses. 2. Europe—Military policy. 3. Anti-tactical ballistic missiles—
Europe. I. Institute for Foreign Policy Analysis. II. Title. III. Series: Special report (Institute
for Foreign Policy Analysis)
UA646.D38 1986   358'.174   86-30349
ISBN 0-08-035175-1

First Printing 1986

Printed by Corporate Press, Inc., Washington, D.C.

Regional Security and Anti-Tactical Ballistic Missiles:
Political and Technical Issues

William A. Davis, Jr.

INSTITUTE FOR FOREIGN POLICY ANALYSIS, INC.
IN ASSOCIATION WITH THE FLETCHER SCHOOL OF LAW AND DIPLOMACY, TUFTS UNIVERSITY

PERGAMON-BRASSEY'S

Institute for Foreign Policy Analysis, Inc.
in association with The Fletcher School of Law and Diplomacy, Tufts University

The Institute for Foreign Policy Analysis, Inc., is an independent, nonpartisan research organization, whose major purposes are to conduct research, publish studies, convene seminars and conferences, strengthen education, and train policy analysts in the field of foreign policy and national security affairs. The Institute maintains a core staff of international relations specialists at its offices in Cambridge, Massachusetts, and Washington, D.C.; draws upon the expertise of scholars, scientists, journalists, businessmen, and other foreign affairs experts; supports a specialized library of periodicals, books, and information files for the use of scholars, students, and the general public; and awards fellowships and research assistantships to promising graduate students.

This study of the political and technical dimensions of anti-tactical ballistic missile (ATBM) systems development by the United States is one of a series of Special Reports on Foreign Policy and National Security addressed to current and emerging issues of critical importance and published on a "quick reaction" basis. The series contains sufficient scope for treatment of all major issue areas of U.S. foreign policy and world affairs.

The Institute for Foreign Policy Analysis, Inc., incorporated in the Commonwealth of Massachusetts, is a tax-exempt organization under Section 501(c)(3) of the U.S. Internal Revenue Code, and has been granted status as a publicly-supported, nonprivate organization under Section 509(a)(1). Contributions to the Institute are tax-deductible.

Main Office: Central Plaza Building, Tenth Floor,
675 Massachusetts Avenue,
Cambridge, Massachusetts 02139-3396.

Washington, D.C., Office: 1612 K Street, N.W., Suite 1204,
Washington, D.C. 20006.

Contents

Summary Overview

The first anti-tactical ballistic missile (ATBM) system program, the Plato project, was started in 1951. It was a product of a fecund period of rocket and guided missile development at the Army's Redstone Arsenal in Huntsville, Alabama. During the 1950s, many advanced weapons and space concepts were spawned at this technical center, largely as a result of the transfer of Wernher von Braun and his team there in 1948. While the space initiative, leading to the launching of the Free World's first satellite, was the most celebrated contribution of this center, there were many other major initiatives in tactical missiles, air defense, strategic ballistic missiles, and ballistic missile defense. ATBM was related to air and ballistic missile defense (BMD), and its early history was intertwined with these weapons concepts. Plato embodied many innovative techniques for engagement of tactical ballistic missiles; however, its lack of mobility and survivability in the field army environment led to the termination of development in 1958.

The next major ATBM system program was the Field Army Ballistic Missile Defense System (FABMDS)*. Started in 1961, it was the first of four generations of systems which became trapped in a web of systems analysis from which they could not be extricated to enter engineering development. These were FABMDS, AADS-70, SAM-D, and Patriot, the latter system finally breaking through the barriers to full-scale engineering development, but not before several "near-death" delays and protracted reviews.

The principal reason for the long period of indecision concerning the next-generation air defense and ATBM system was the influence of Secretary McNamara's emphasis on systems analysis, paper studies, and the illusory goal of eliminating all risk before starting development. In contrast to the productive period of the 1950s at the Army's Redstone Arsenal, it became virtually impossible to clear all of the hurdles leading to the start of development and the ultimate deployment of new systems. Contributing to this period of indecision was a pronounced ambivalence toward ATBM: It was initially the sole objective of FABMDS; then air defense was added to the FABMDS requirements; it persisted as a joint requirement through AADS-70 and into SAM-D; then it was canceled from SAM-D; and, finally, ATBM was reinstated in Patriot. This checkered history

---

* A glossary of acronyms used in this Special Report can be found on page 48.

of ATBM is probably attributable to a combination of factors, including doubts about the seriousness of the tactical ballistic missile (TBM) threat, skepticism about the technical feasibility of solving the threat with a mobile system, economic constraints, and, in later years, the influence of the ABM Treaty.

Preceding the start of the FABMDS project in 1961, and continuing sporadically thereafter, there were a number of tests and studies of the ATBM capabilities of existing air defense systems, notably Hawk, Nike-Hercules, and Mauler. In January 1960, a Hawk missile intercepted an Honest John ballistic rocket at White Sands Missile Range and achieved a nonnuclear kill of the target. Subsequently, additional firings of Hawk and Nike-Hercules were conducted against ballistic targets including the longer-range Corporal and Sergeant systems. Studies were conducted on the capabilities of these two fielded systems and the developmental system, Mauler, against a wide range of ballistic missiles, and consideration was given to minor and major modifications to these systems. Generally, these air defense systems were found to have limited capabilities against tactical ballistic missiles when measured against the requirements for nonnuclear kill, mobility, and affordable technical modifications.

The subject of ATBM was relatively quiescent for several years following Plato and FABMDS, and the studies and experiments on air defense systems, until the creation of an ATM office in Missile Command (MICOM) in the early 1980s, and the concurrent reinstatement of an ATBM requirement for Patriot. (The abbreviation to "ATM" connotes a broader requirement to include defense against cruise missiles.) More recently, a major surge in ATBM emphasis has occurred under the auspices of the Strategic Defense Initiative (SDI) program and through the Army's Strategic Defense Command; and a number of allied nations and companies have become actively involved in ATBM architecture studies and technology programs. In addition, the MICOM ATBM activity has increased under a newly created Joint Tactical Missile Defense Project Office. The scale and breadth of ATBM activity is greater than ever before, impelled by the growing Soviet tactical ballistic missile threat, including increasingly accurate conventional capabilities. The Soviets have also developed an ATBM system, the SA-X-12, which is estimated to be close to deployment. One of the great challenges presented by the widespread participation in allied ATBM studies is to coordinate the findings effectively and arrive at a consensus on approaches to system solutions.

The European perspectives on ATBM include a number of arguments against development and deployment, most of which are related to the opposition to SDI. In the literature from European sources, the following arguments against strategic defense and ATBM are the most common:

- Defense runs counter to the doctrine of Mutual Assured Destruction (MAD) and is therefore destabilizing.

- U.S. strategic defense would give rise to a "fortress America" complex and tend to decouple U.S. and European allied security interests.

- SDI threatens the ABM Treaty, and ATBM cannot be deployed without violating the treaty.

- Strategic defense makes conventional war more likely.

- If defense is not 100 percent effective, it is worthless.

- Extended deterrence will be eroded by defense.

- Flexible response will be impaired by defense.

Many Europeans cling to the doctrine of MAD—now perceived to be threatened by the emphasis on defense—with a fervor equal to that of U.S. adherents to this doctrine. They believe that it supports a deterrence policy that has successfully prevented nuclear war for forty years; therefore, we should not abandon a proven doctrine for a transition to one that places more reliance on strategic defense. What is missing in this view is a recognition that MAD has been seriously eroded as an enforceable doctrine and that defense can, in the interim transitional period, restore the credibility of deterrence based on MAD. At the strategic level, defense can protect our retaliatory forces to assure the capability to respond to a Soviet first strike. At the tactical level, defense can protect NATO assets required to implement the flexible response doctrine. What is compelling about both of these defense missions is the unmistakable presence of the threat: the Soviet strategic missile threat to the survivability of our strategic retaliatory forces and the Soviet tactical missile threat to NATO forces.

The decoupling argument would seem to apply only to strategic defense of the Continental United States (CONUS) and not to ATBM, but the opponents of defense are frequently indiscriminate in the application of such arguments. Defense in any form is often seen as a diminution of U.S. resolve to invoke a nuclear response to Soviet aggression in Western Europe. In this regard, the decoupling argument is related to the fears that defense will conflict with flexible response and extended deterrence. The perceived conflict between defense and flexible response is based largely on the concern that defense will restore the credibility of the intermediate levels of response and thereby make the strategic nuclear response more remote. Many Europeans prefer a state of deterrence based on pure assured destruction and the threat of direct escalation to the nuclear level; ATBM is seen as an instrument that will localize the battleground to Western Europe and raise the threshold for strategic nuclear intervention. Strategic defense is viewed by European critics in the frame of reference of the ultimate "Star Wars" scenario when nuclear weapons are rendered "impotent and obsolete," rather than in the intermediate role of enhancing deterrence based on the threat of retaliation. From this perspective, fears are proclaimed that a new strategy of defense dominance is dawning which will weaken the nuclear guarantee embodied in extended deterrence. This perspective, which sees the United States ensconced in a secure sanctuary that is not accessible to the allies, is also behind the decoupling argument.

With respect to the ABM Treaty, there are many Europeans who have joined with groups in the United States to attempt to stretch the treaty to prohibit ATBM. On the face of it, there is nothing in the treaty which is relevant to ATBM, since the treaty is a bilateral agreement limiting defenses against strategic ballistic missiles in the territories of the two signatories. However, a compex web of extreme interpretations, gray areas, and questionable actions has been constructed by opponents of SDI and ATBM. Those who are attempting to stretch the ABM Treaty to prohibit ATBM usually use Articles VI and IX in their arguments. Article VI prohibits giving components other than ABM components a capability to counter *strategic* ballistic missiles, an exclusion intended to prevent the upgrading of air defense systems to achieve this capability; and Article IX prohibits the transfer of *ABM systems or their components* to other states. Until recently, there was no serious support for the view that designing systems such as Patriot (and its predecessor, SAM-D) and the Soviet SA-X-12 system to have a capability against the full range of tactical ballistic missiles violates the ABM Treaty.

Curiously, there is now more concern expressed, in both the United States and Europe, about the treaty implications of the nascent allied efforts in ATBM than about the soon-to-be-deployed SA-X-12. As a practical matter, the only means of enforcing and verifying the restriction of Article VI is through the restriction on "testing in an ABM mode." The Soviets have apparently complied with this restriction on testing with their SA-X-12 system, and there is no doubt that the United States and the allies will follow suit when and if they reach the testing phase with an ATBM system.

The other arguments directed against ATBM are addressed in the main body of this report; they will not be summarized here except in the context of a final observation about the false premise of the entire body of criticism.

viii

That is, the main thrust of the arguments against ATBM, and strategic defense in general, are based on the false premise that it would be an initiative that would upset the current balance and trigger an unwanted response on the part of the Soviet Union. In point of fact, the exact opposite is true. *The compelling case for defense is as a response to Soviet actions which have created serious imbalances.* These Soviet actions are: (1) deployment of a counterforce capability against U.S. land-based ICBMs which weakens deterrence and extended deterrence and which can be offset with active defense; (2) deployment of INF and short-range tactical ballistic missiles which threaten to take out key NATO military targets in a preemptive first strike and which can be countered by deployment of a treaty-compliant ATBM system; and (3) development and imminent deployment of an ATBM system—establishing a precedent under the ABM Treaty—capable of engaging allied tactical ballistic missiles and thus creating an imbalance which can be corrected by reciprocal allied ATBM deployment.

The unilateral, destabilizing actions by the Soviets, enumerated above, can be met by defenses which are technologically advanced, including the use of nonnuclear warheads. It has been demonstrated that nonnuclear warheads are effective against ballistic missiles, first by the Homing Overlay Experiment (HOE) against exoatmospheric warheads in 1984 and then by the Short Range HIT (or FLAG) experiment against endoatmospheric warheads.

The Soviet tactical ballistic missile threat is composed of four systems covering the spectrum from the 120-kilometer-range SS-21 to the 5000-kilometer, MIRVed SS-20 system. The critical parameter for short-range ballistic missiles that determines their efficacy for nonnuclear missions is accuracy. The reported improvements in the accuracy of the three Soviet short-range missiles has given rise to a new concern about the use of this class of missile (notably, the position taken by West German Defense Minister Manfred Woerner) against discrete military targets. The unclassified estimates of CEPs (circular error probabilities) for these short-range missiles vary widely, from a few tens of meters to a few hundreds of meters. This spread in accuracy estimates makes the difference between a very substantial nonnuclear capability and an almost negligible one, and strongly indicates that a clearer consensus is needed before the severity of this threat can be agreed upon. However, there can be no disagreement on the destructive potential, indeed, the overkill capacity, of the Soviet tactical nuclear missiles, or on the incapacitating capability of their stockpile of chemical warheads.

There are several features of the TBM threat which pose stressing problems for an ATBM system: potentially the most severe may be the lethality of the nonnuclear defensive interceptor warhead used to engage conventional, chemical, and nuclear offensive warheads—with the chemical as the most difficult to counter. On the other hand, the TBM threat in some respects poses a less stressing problem to a defense system than the strategic ballistic missile threat: probably the most important of these features are the lower anticipated local traffic density and the less sophisticated penetration aids likely to be encountered by the ATBM system.

A crucial question hanging over the current surge of interest in ATBM is: What threat should an ATBM system be designed to counter? This question has special relevance to nuclear-armed tactical missiles in general and the SS-20 in particular. In apparent deference to the imputed constraints of the ABM Treaty, the SS-20 has been strangely missing from official statements on ATBM requirements. Moreover, the advent of effective nonnuclear tactical missiles has been emphasized so strongly that the massive tactical nuclear threat has been virtually ignored in ATBM discussions. This trend in Atlantic Alliance thought seems to ignore two facts: that a defense system cannot technically distinguish between nuclear and nonnuclear warheads, and that it is not feasible to assure treaty compliance by arbitrarily placing a range limit on tactical missiles that can be engaged. In order for an ATBM system to be effective against both nuclear and nonnuclear warheads, it must be designed with a "keep-out" capability against nuclear warheads; it cannot be designed for nonnuclear missiles and at the same time be effective against nuclear missiles. With respect to the question of a range cutoff, such as designing a system to counter missiles with a smaller range than the SS-20, it is possible that such a system could be made to be demonstrably ineffective against the SS-20 in defense of soft targets and still be effective against long-range strategic missiles in defense of hard targets. This illustrates the futility of basing treaty compliance on design limitations and leads to the conclusion, again, that the only practical criterion for determining compliance is the provision of "testing in an ABM mode."

The trajectories for tactical ballistic missiles dictate, to a large extent, the type of defense systems which can be used to engage them. As shown in Figure 1, only the SS-20 trajectory is exoatmospheric for a large fraction of its flight path; therefore, it is the only system which can be confidently engaged by space-based or exoatmospheric defense components. It is possible that some space-based weapons may ultimately be able to penetrate into the atmosphere to reach these short-range missiles, but the natural near-term solution is to use terminal and late-midcourse components. Air defense systems, such as Patriot, can be upgraded to engage the lower end of the threat spectrum. SDI elements, such as HEDI, TIR, ERIS, and AOA, can be applied to the ATBM problem, but they are overdesigned for this class of target, and their use in this role introduces treaty compliance issues. The ideal solution is to design and deploy a dedicated ATBM system.

The current U.S. strategic defense program should place greater emphasis on the accelerated development of an advanced terminal system prototype, suitable for both an ATBM capability and for defense of hardened military targets in the continental United States. A mobile terminal defense system can be developed which can perform both missions effectively and thus provide economies in the development investment required. The system could be deployed for the ATBM mission within the terms of the ABM Treaty, and it could serve as a rapidly deployable hedge option for the CONUS hardsite mission. To assure compliance with Article VI of the treaty, the system should be tested against Pershing and Lance targets, but not against strategic missile targets. It would not be necessary to make an ATBM deployment decision before embarking on a development program; the important initial decision is to develop a complete, integrated prototype system so as to minimize deployment leadtime.

The development of such a versatile terminal defense system would respond to all three of the destabilizing Soviet initiatives outlined above: the counterforce first-strike force, tactical ballistic missile deployment, and the SA-X-12 ATBM system.

The characteristics of an advanced, multi-mission terminal defense system would be similar to those of the LoAD/Sentry system, the BMD system developed for several years and then canceled in 1984. The radar would operate at a high microwave frequency, optimized for operation in a severe ECM environment, with high resolution, and with road mobility. It would be designed to provide the maximum power-aperture product achievable, consistent with road mobility. With this design approach, the upper end of the spectrum of tactical ballistic missiles would be engageable, including the SS-20, with some overlap with upgraded air defense systems at the lower end of the spectrum. The interceptor would be designed to operate with homing guidance and a nonnuclear warhead for the ATBM mission and with command guidance and a nuclear warhead for the CONUS hardsite mission.

For both roles of the terminal defense system sketched above, plans should be made from the outset of development to integrate the system at a later date with other tiers of SDI. In particular, the coupling between the terminal system and a late-midcourse (ERIS/AOA) overlay should be thought through in advance. For some ATBM objectives, it would be desirable to deploy a two-tier layered defense (this would be in a breakout mode if SDI components are used, beyond the limits of the ABM Treaty).

The low leakage provided by such a layered system is needed for very high priority targets, such as command headquarters. In addition, the large coverage of a late-midcourse system is attractive from a cost point of view and, particularly, for engagement of the SS-20. The exoatmospheric overlay system can be used only for the SS-20, but it is the ideal solution for that missile. In CONUS, the proposed terminal system could serve as the bottom rung in a "full-up" SDI architecture; considered in an evolutionary context, it could be used effectively for missions such as SAC base defense along with the late-midcourse tier.

A prudent approach to defense against the tactical ballistic missile threat would be, first, to deploy a dedicated terminal system, in conjunction with upgraded air defense systems, for defense of the highest priority military targets in NATO, and then expand the system as the situation requires. Such an early terminal system deployment, when combined with passive measures and counterbattery tactics, would relieve the critical vulnerabilities of the NATO force structure, enhance deterrence, and restore the credibility of flexible response. A relatively modest deployment of terminal batteries could protect the highest priority targets, and with a concerted prototype development program, an IOC (initial operating capability) in the mid-1990s could be met. Growth of the defense could proceed along a number of alternative paths: a particularly attractive growth option is to add an optical adjunct sensor, capable of handing over to the terminal radar. An optical adjunct for a handover mode can increase the detection range of the radar and expand the footprint of a terminal system significantly. Ultimately, a two-tier ATBM system, the terminal system with an exoatmospheric overlay for the SS-20 threat, appears to be the most robust solution to the threat.

The technology is in hand, or within reach in the near term, to solve the threat posed by tactical ballistic missiles. The most critical set of technologies for this mission are those related to endoatmospheric nonnuclear kill: active millimeter wave homing, fuzing, warhead lethality, rapid interceptor response time, and kill assessment. Promising recent progress in these technologies lends confidence that a system prototype development program can begin immediately. There is no need to await the results of studies for two or three years. If an intensive prototype development program is carried out, this menacing and destabilizing threat can be met in the 1990s.

1. ATBM Origins

Relationship to Strategic Defense and Air Defense

The origin of anti-tactical ballistic missile (ATBM) concepts, as with many other rocket and guided missile concepts, is traceable to a creative period in the 1950s at the Army's Redstone Arsenal in Huntsville, Alabama. Thanks to the impetus created by the transfer of the Wernher von Braun Peenemunde team from Fort Bliss to Huntsville in 1948, many advanced space and weapons concepts were spawned at Redstone over the ensuing decade. The best known aspect of this fertile period was the space initiative, which first found expression in a pre-Sputnik proposal to launch an artificial earth satellite using available military hardware. As space history now records, it was not until after the shock of Sputnik and the failure of the Navy Vanguard program that the Army was given approval to launch the Free World's first satellite on January 31, 1958. While this event put the Army missile center in Huntsville "on the map," there were other branches of missilery that were to grow into significant national defense programs. These included strategic ballistic missiles, tactical missiles, air defense, and ballistic missile defense.

Ballistic missile defense was an outgrowth of air defense, specifically the Nike family of air defense systems which began in the 1953-1955 timeframe. In fact, early studies of ballistic missile defense were combined with air defense missions. The first such study was Project Thumper, begun in the mid-1940s, whose objectives were to investigate the feasibility of a high-altitude anti-aircraft missile and the potential of creating a defense against the V-2 surface-to-surface guided missile. In March 1955, the Army contracted with the Bell Telephone Laboratories (BTL) of the Western Electric Corporation to conduct an 18-month study of a forward-looking defense of the "Zone of the Interior" against both the air-breathing threat and ICBMs. This study, originally called Nike II, was changed by the Army in June 1955 when it placed primary emphasis on the ICBM threat, while continuing to investigate the air-breathing threat. The dual role of air defense and ballistic missile defense was retained in Nike II, featuring a missile with interchangeable "noses" for both homing and command guidance, up until the Nike-Zeus development contract was signed in February 1957. At this point the air defense role was dropped and the strategic BMD path remained separate and distinct from air defense in all future programs.

The early formative period of ballistic missile defense included consideration of both tactical ballistic missiles and strategic ballistic missiles. The latter mission was much more prominent in both the scale of the programs and the level of national attention because of the difficulty of defending against long-range strategic missiles and the important implications of achieving such a defensive capability. Furthermore, the inter-Service rivalry for the challenging strategic mission was fiercely fought, creating many headlines, while the Army proceeded quietly with the uncontested tactical mission. It was not until the McElroy decision of January 1958 that the Army was assigned the strategic BMD mission, with the go-ahead for operational development of Nike-Zeus. For many years prior to this decision the ATBM problem had been investigated, and it was to become a subject of sporadic study, but with no sustained development, for the next twenty-five years.

The Plato project[1] was the first program dedicated to defense against tactical ballistic missiles. Started in 1951 and continued until 1958, it featured the use of an interceptor missile configuration that had extended aerodynamic surfaces, a large acquisition radar, and a triangulation radar for precision target tracking. The Plato system design represented a triumph of engineering excellence over practical utility in a tactical battlefield environment. The acquisition radar antenna for Plato was over one hundred feet in length, and the triangulation tracking system was composed of dozens of antennas spread over a baseline of tens of miles. The large number of powerful dish radars promised to provide elegant solutions to the problems of acquiring and precisely tracking the position of a ballistic vehicle, but at the sacrifice of mobility and survivability.

The next major ATBM program was the Field Army Ballistic Missile Defense System (FABMDS).[2] It was started in 1961 when competitive study contracts were awarded to three major aerospace contractors. The original rationale for FABMDS was to fill the gap in field army protection against ballistic missiles, as had already been done against aircraft with air defense systems such as Nike-Hercules, Hawk, Redeye, and Mauler. The FABMDS design concepts profited greatly from the evolution of technology in the decade following the inception of Plato. The contrasts between Plato and FABMDS system designs were comparable to those between Nike-Zeus and Nike-X in the strategic defense arena; the advent of phased-array radar technology and solid-state electronics led to greatly improved

---

[1] U.S. Army White Sands Signal Corps Agency, *Survey of Guidance Systems* (4th Edition), Volume I, prepared by Gilfillan Bros., Contract DA36-039-SC-70109, March 31, 1957.

[2] Raytheon Company, *Summary Field Army Ballistic Missile Defense System (FABMDS) Final Study Report*, Volume I, BR-1234A, Department of the Army Contract DA-19-020-ORD-53355, July 10, 1961.

effectiveness against large threats and more reliable component designs. However, the optimization of the FABMDS system for ATBM was compromised in 1962 when the Qualitative Materiel Requirement (QMR) for that system was amended to add the requirement for an air defense capability.[3] By this time, the design concepts for ATBM were well developed and it was difficult to add air defense capability without major redesign. For this, and other reasons, FABMDS was phased out in 1963 in favor of a more balanced approach to the dual missions.

FABMDS was the first in a long series of short-lived air defense and ATBM concepts extending through AADS-70, SAM-D, and Patriot—a period of remarkable decline in the productivity of weapons systems development. It was a protracted period of study, redefinition, start-stop programming, and general drifting within the air defense community. The dominant activity of this period was systems analysis, the pernicious practice ushered in by the McNamara era in the Defense Department, which substituted paper studies for hardware development and clogged the pipeline of new weapons systems for many years. Although Patriot finally stabilized into a full-scale development and deployment program, it and the predecessor SAM-D program were plagued by many near-death delays and Patriot's technology was subjected to needless risks of obsolescence.

It is interesting to contrast the period depicted above with the earlier years at Redstone Arsenal. In the earlier period, extending through the decade of the 1950s, it was a relatively smooth process to evolve from studies into full-scale development and then into production. In my own experience on the Hawk project from 1956 to 1960, the program moved ahead with remarkable ease from one phase to the next, including a relatively routine approval by Secretary of Defense Wilson to go into production. Because of this unimpeded process, new weapons systems were pouring out of the pipeline at a steady rate. While these systems were certainly flawed, and the early Hawk system was no exception, the procedures in place at the time allowed for effective corrective action, rework, retrofits, and system upgrades. A fatal misconception of the McNamara faith in systems analysis was that all pitfalls could be anticipated, and all of the bugs removed, before hardware development began. What this period of "paralysis by analysis" in air defense demonstrated, along with many other lessons which are too involved to treat here, was that the studies frequently addressed the wrong problems, and the real problems did not surface until development got under way. Hence, the

---

[3] William A. Davis, Jr., and John A. French, "CONUS Low Altitude Air Defense," Presentation to General Dick, Headquarters, Army Air Defense Command (ARADCOM), August 21, 1962.

economies promised by the practice of analyzing all of the options and contingencies before starting development were never realized; in fact, the total cost of development became much greater, no new systems were introduced, and the resultant mounds of study reports were of marginal relevance.

Throughout the four generations of air defense systems cited above, the concept of a joint ATBM role was adopted and dropped on a number of occasions. As previously described, the FABMDS system gave precedence to the ATBM role and added air defense after initial concept definition. During the AADS-70 period and well into the SAM-D development program, ATBM was a joint requirement along with air defense. During the SAM-D development program, the requirement for ATBM was dropped in order to reduce cost. Recently, a limited requirement for ATBM has been added to Patriot. The Patriot requirement is essentially for a self-defense capability against the lower end of the TBM threat spectrum. Reflecting back on this twenty-five-year period of history, the severity of the tactical missile threat at the time does not appear to have justified the priority of the ATBM effort represented by Plato and FABMDS, but the more recent growth of the TBM threat raises doubts that ATBM should have been dropped from SAM-D.

It is difficult to sort out the causes for the checkered history of Army ATBM development—for the start-stop cycles and the failure of all ATBM initiatives to be sustained long enough to evolve into a significant development state. The most recent example of this was the creation, with considerable promise for reinvigorating this mission field, of an ATM office in the U.S. Army Missile Command several years ago. That office never seemed to receive the priority and impetus needed to get a serious program going, and it withered into a skeleton operation with little visible impact. It has now been replaced by the Joint Tactical Missile Defense Project Office, with renewed priority and an increased budget. In addition, the SDI program has launched a theater defense program aimed at the definition of ATBM architectures, and it has also funded similar programs in allied countries. It is too early to determine whether these SDI and MICOM initiatives will progress further than previous ATBM programs, but the severity of the threat and the scale of the program bode well for a more enduring effort. There appear to be several reasons why ATBM has never materialized into a sustained development program: a perception that tactical missiles would never become a serious threat to the field army; a judgment that the technology could not provide an effective and field-worthy counter to the threat; competition for development dollars; and ambiguities surrounding the ABM Treaty and ATBM development (there was a conspicuous tendency not to talk about an ATBM capability for

SAM-D and Patriot for a long period following the signing of the ABM Treaty in 1972).

Early Tests and Ad Hoc Studies

In January 1960, a Hawk missile intercepted an Honest John rocket over White Sands Missile Range and decisively killed the target with a non-nuclear warhead. This was probably the first successful intercept of a ballistic missile, pre-dating the first successful Nike-Zeus intercept of an ICBM by over two years (not that the Hawk engagement of a short-range rocket was as significant as the intercept of an ICBM). As an engineer working in the Hawk project office—one of five engineers in the office at that time—I was involved in this mission and remember some of the strange events surrounding its accomplishment.

The Hawk mission to engage an Honest John ballistic missile was very loosely and informally planned, as were many events during this period in missile development history. We had received a teletype in the Hawk project office in December 1959 from the Office Chief of Ordnance in Washington requesting that we schedule firings of the Hawk missile against ballistic targets such as the Honest John. I visited White Sands Missile Range in January 1960 to arrange the first mission and encountered a problem in securing allocation of an Honest John rocket and range approval for shooting a Hawk at such a free-flight target. Working with the Raytheon prime contractor team on Hawk, we had readied the Hawk missile which was poised on its three-missile launcher waiting for the button to be pushed. The problem with obtaining the Honest John was related to range safety, the denial of accuracy measurements if the vehicle was intercepted, and a general aversion of the Honest John project people to having their vehicle shot at. In a series of telephone conversations with various military and civilian employees at White Sands, I somehow obtained permission, with a leadtime of hours, to engage a planned Honest John firing. The mission went off smoothly, admittedly with the benefit to Hawk of shared, simultaneous countdowns. The Honest John was shattered by the Hawk blast-fragmentation warhead and much of the debris was recovered from the desert floor. (I still have one of the pieces from the Honest John, mounted on an inscribed momento of the occasion.)

It was a very fortuitous event that we had excellent photographic coverage of the Hawk intercept of the Honest John. I was instructed by my superiors at Redstone Arsenal to wait at White Sands until the film was developed for the mission and to hand-carry a copy back to Huntsville. I brought back the classified color film coverage of the mission and displayed it

5

in conference rooms for cleared personnel working in the development organization. I was to learn very shortly after this how quickly the priority for publicity can override the requirements for security classification. Within a few days, the film coverage was shown on the CBS Evening News.

Over the next several years, a number of Hawk and Nike-Hercules air defense missiles were successfully fired at ballistic targets, including the longer-range Corporal and Sergeant vehicles. Generally, these missions proved that technical issues such as missile guidance and control and warhead fuzing could be solved for ballistic targets. However, the tactical significance of the missions was limited because the time of arrival and the direction of the targets were known in advance and the environment for the missions was controlled.

The serious significance of the early Hawk missions was that a defense system employing homing guidance could perform a nonnuclear kill of a tactical ballistic missile. Twenty-six years later, there is a requirement for performing this mission with a nonnuclear warhead, and an implied requirement for the use of homing guidance, either passive, semi-active (as in the case of the Hawk), or active. Only recently has the technology emerged, with the successful testing of the Short-Range HIT (homing interceptor technology) system, to perform active radar homing on ballistic targets.

Concurrently with the ATBM experiments at White Sands, a number of ad hoc studies were carried out in the early 1960s to determine the capabilities and limitations of air defense systems to fill the ATBM role. These studies concentrated on systems already in the field or well into development, such as Hawk, Nike-Hercules, and Mauler, as opposed to the "next-generation" air defense system which started with FABMDS and evolved, as described above, through three major generations and numerous smaller excursions before entering into a development program. The earliest study of this type was one I was assigned to lead, which called for a brief examination of the capabilities of air defense systems, with and without modifications, to engage tactical ballistic missiles.[4] (I retrieved and reviewed a report of this ancient study from the Redstone Scientific Information Center in preparation for this monograph.) This study analyzed air defense system effectiveness in terms of defended areas, traffic handling capability, and kill probabilities against U.S. tactical ballistic missiles (as a substitute for Soviet missiles, which were more difficult to characterize). The tactical missiles considered were Honest John, Ser-

---

[4] Army Rocket and Guided Missile Agency (ARGMA), *Evaluation of Anti-Missile Capabilities of Hawk, Nike-Hercules, and Mauler*, May 13, 1960.

geant, and Redstone, providing about an order-of-magnitude spread of ranges from approximately 15 to 150 nautical miles. The modifications considered for the air defense systems were categorized as minor and major, the latter being defined as those entailing the addition of new major items (subsystems) to the system. The technical feasibility of several modifications for each of the three air defense systems was evaluated and cost and schedules for the modifications were estimated.

The study referenced above found that the ATBM capability that can be realized by modifying existing air defense systems is marginal, a conclusion that remains valid today. In general, the main problem in adapting existing air defense systems to this mission is in acquiring and tracking the targets; the air defense missiles are somewhat more adaptable than the acquisition and track radars. Of course, this problem is brought about by the different trajectory, smaller radar cross-section, and higher velocity of tactical missiles as compared to aircraft. In the case of Mauler, the study was more optimistic about a capability against shorter-range tactical missiles because that system was in an early stage of development and it could be more readily modified. However, Mauler, a system in the Roland class, was later canceled because of the difficulty of packaging the system on a single-tracked vehicle; Roland was also canceled, over ten years later, for similar reasons. Hawk was found to have an inherent capability against shorter-range missiles, as demonstrated in the White Sands test, but it needed a completely new acquisition radar to extend its capability up to the longer-range, Redstone class missile. Nike-Hercules was found to have radar power levels and interceptor energy levels compatible with engagement of longer-range missiles, but its command guidance was not consistent with nonnuclear kill, and its subsystems were not mobile.

All of the experimental and study activity of air defense systems in an ATBM role in the 1959-1961 period culminated in the start of FABMDS, briefly described above. This was the new system that was introduced, with considerable fanfare and excitement within the Army, to overcome all of the limitations of air defense systems and to provide the field army with excellent protection against the emerging tactical missile threat. The FABMDS concept was certainly consistent with the findings of the studies of this period, such as the referenced 1950 study, in that it represented an acknowledgment that air defense system upgrades provided only marginal utility against tactical missiles. Again, it is difficult to trace the reasons for the rapid disenchantment with FABMDS, but it is likely that technology hurdles played a major role. As the FABMDS concept was stretched to enable it to reach a level of performance against the longer-range tactical missiles, it encountered many of the challenges of strategic

7

BMD. Many of the same "what if" questions that plagued Nike-Zeus and Nike-X were hurled at FABMDS, and it was encumbered with the additional requirement that it had to be mobile.

There seem to be pronounced cycles in the level of interest manifested in various types of weapon systems, and ATBM provides a striking example of this. Following the intense interest in ATBM sketched above, the subject was relatively quiescent until it resurfaced in the SDI era. The current emphasis is different in many respects, notably because of participation by West European and other allied nations and the growing consensus on the severity of the threat. However, in between these large peaks of interest, separated by an interval of about twenty years, there were recurrent flashes of activity that always faded away as suddenly as they appeared. I participated in a number of "flaps" in the ATBM lull following the redefinition of FABMDS; each "flap" seemed for a brief time to herald a revival of interest in the Pentagon for a serious program. At a greater distance, I witnessed the creation of the Missile Command ATM office cited above and the reinstatement of an ATBM requirement for Patriot. These latter actions were relatively modest precursors to the widespread efforts now being mounted under the sponsorship of the SDI and MICOM programs.

2. The Current ATBM Surge

The current revival of interest in ATBM under the auspices of the Strategic Defense Initiative is a remarkable development, given the dramatic birth of SDI, its lofty goals, and the direction it took following the Defense Technology Study Team (Fletcher Panel) deliberations. SDI was originally formulated as a long-term research program with no vestiges of traditional BMD development or near-term response options, in line with the Fletcher Panel recommendations.[5] It concentrated on the challenging mission of defending cities with near-perfect levels of defense and a heavy dependence on space-based weapons. The less difficult mission of defending military targets, for which traditional BMD approaches are feasible and ideally suited, was relegated to the back burner, if not entirely abandoned. With the nascent SDI Theater Defense Program, as the ATBM program is called, an element of more traditional BMD systems and technology will inevitably be infused into the SDI program along with a tactical dimension.

The first signs of a potential ATBM initiative could be seen in the Army part of SDI about two years ago. The Army has been carrying out a long-term study called the Systems Requirements Study (SRS) in Huntsville for more than two years, and this study early on began revisiting the requirements for theater defense, as well as CONUS defense. The SRS is a substantial ad hoc effort involving a large number of contractors and government agencies. It has generated large volumes of data on the threat, mission analysis, technology requirements, system design trade-offs, and all of the other issues associated with theater defense. This study clearly illuminated the threat posed by tactical ballistic missiles, particularly against targets in NATO, and it pointed out in considerable technical detail the potential solutions to this threat.

No attempt will be made here to trace the details of the SDI decision-making process, but it is clear that the findings of the SRS and the desire to find a mechanism for European participation in SDI were factors in the launching of the Theater Defense Program. SRS has uncovered the need for several new components in SDI, notably a low endoatmospheric defense interceptor (LEDI) and a mobile ground-based radar (GBR), in order to perform the ATBM mission. At one point, a notice appeared in the *Commerce Business Daily* (CBD) of an intention to embark on an LED program

---

[5] See William A. Davis, Jr., *Asymmetries in U.S. and Soviet Strategic Defense Programs: Implications for Near-Term American Deployment Options* (Cambridge, Mass.: Institute for Foreign Policy Analysis, Special Report, 1986), pp.1-14.

9

(by this time, the "I" had been dropped from LEDI in deference to those who favored inclusion of ground-based electromagnetic launchers as well as conventional interceptors). This procurement was delayed, apparently in order to allow time to work out arrangements for European participation and to develop a plan for a Theater Defense Architecture Study before any new component developments were started. Meanwhile, negotiations proceeded with European allies for agreements to participate in SDI, and Memorandums of Understanding have now been signed with the United Kingdom and the Federal Republic of Germany. While these agreements pertain to SDI research across-the-board, the creation of a Theater Defense Program, primarily aimed at defense of assets in NATO-Europe, was likely seen as a way to enrich the cooperative developments and to provide "ground-floor" opportunities for jointly addressing a troubling new Soviet threat.

A significant procurement was announced in the CBD on June 6, 1986, entitled "Architecture Study for Theater Defense." This announcement was an unusually lengthy synopsis of a planned procurement, reflecting a streamlined approach to the study which by-passed a formal Request for Proposal and invited direct bids by firms in the United States and allied countries. The announcement solicited proposals on evolutionary architecture concepts to "negate the theater missile threat with primary emphasis on short-range ballistic missiles (SRBMs)." It defined two phases of the study, extending over an eighteen-month period, with a down-select process after the first six months. It spelled out eight technical requirements for Phase I, consisting of a classical study process—such as definition of missions and functions and evaluation of effectiveness, very similar to the process followed on SRS. While the cruise missile threat was not specifically mentioned, the bidders were requested to identify the benefits to be derived from architectures defined against the air-breathing threat. A curious omission from the threat definition was the Soviet SS-20 INF missile, a prominent part of the threat studied in the SRS.

In response to the above procurement announcement, a number of contractor teams have been formed, composed of companies in the United States and allied countries. There are perhaps ten to twelve teams in the process of writing proposals for Phase I of the study, and at least seven allied countries are participating. This unprecedented degree of "mating" among the United States and foreign countries will undoubtedly entail many problems of security, technology transfer, and treaty compliance.

In addition to the SDI-sponsored Theater Defense Study, through the Army's Strategic Defense Command, there are a number of parallel ATBM studies in progress in other countries. The United Kingdom has been given a $10 million grant by the SDI Office to perform an independent theater architecture study, and it is expected that Israel and perhaps several other countries will receive similar grants. The Federal Republic of Germany is investing on the order of $17 million from its own defense appropriations for ATBM study and development. There is also a study under way by NATO's Advisory Group for Aerospace Research and Development (AGARD) on the ATBM subject. Taken together, this is the most massive concentration of effort ever applied to ATBM; indeed, it is difficult to think of any one defense mission that has received such intensive international study. The main problem will be how to coordinate all of these studies.

It was apparent with the SRS study that there is a tendency when there are a lot of "players" to get a lot of different answers. If the scope and diversity of SRS is multiplied by several orders of magnitude, one can imagine how many divergent and conflicting approaches to ATBM will emerge from all of the ongoing studies. Moreover, it does not appear possible to exercise very tight coordination over the many different international groups conducting these studies. Fierce nationalist pride, divergent regional perspectives, treaty constraints, and technology transfer issues will be added to the normal competitive environment. All of this suggests that there will be a "moment of truth" about two years from now, when all of the study results are in, when hard decisions will need to be made, and when the authority for making such decisions will be diffuse.

3. European Perspectives

The Arguments Against Defense

As noted above, there is increasing activity in European and other allied countries on ATBM. However, there is also opposition to ATBM and SDI, as there is in this country. A search through the literature over the past several years on European attitudes toward defense, much of it from European sources, turns up several common arguments against defense. Some of these are the same as we hear in the United States, but others are peculiar to European and NATO outlooks. There are various shades of opposition opinion, depending on whether the subject is SDI or EDI, strategic defense or ATBM, or whether both the United States and the USSR deploy strategic defenses or only one side deploys them. However, the following general opposition themes, not mutually exclusive, are the most prevalent:

- **Defense runs counter to the doctrine of Mutual Assured Destruction and is therefore destabilizing.** One related argument holds that SDI will result in the militarization of space and thereby introduce a new threat to strategic stability, and that it will induce an offense-defense arms spiral. These concerns are probably the most widespread and deep-seated, and they correspond closely with the central opposition in the United States.

- **U.S. strategic defense would give rise to a new "fortress America" complex and tend to decouple U.S. and European allied security interests.** This is an argument which does not find much support in the United States, but it has been vigorously expressed by high-level officials in Europe.

- **SDI threatens the ABM Treaty, and ATBM cannot be deployed without violating the treaty.** The view that SDI, even in the research phase, opposes the spirit of the treaty is probably more widely held, but a few spokesmen contend that the treaty actually prohibits ATBM.

- **Strategic defense makes conventional war more likely.** This argument also spills over into the ATBM arena because it holds that, if tactical missiles are nullified—just as if strategic missiles are nullified—by defense then the battleground shifts to conventional warfare.

- **If defense is not 100 percent effective, it is worthless.** This has, in various formulations, been a central argument against SDI in the United States.

- **INF modernization should be reconsidered in the light of ATBM.** This argument is usually advanced with the question: Why do we have to replicate Soviet INF forces if we can defend against them?

- **Extended deterrence will be eroded by defense.** This argument is applied most frequently to the case where the Soviets have strategic defenses; however, it is also applied to instances where the United States has a strategic defense capability or where both sides are defended.

- **Flexible response will be impaired by defense.** This argument is related to the one on extended deterrence, but it is applied to even lower levels of escalation.

Clinging to Mutual Assured Destruction

Hubertus G. Hoffman has written that the doctrine of Mutual Assured Destruction (MAD) "was attractive to Europeans, both philosophically and psychologically, because it not only connoted a territorial vulnerability of the United States comparable (if not equal) to the military exposedness of Western Europe, but actually enshrined this vulnerability in doctrinal terms."[6] Hoffman was formerly a member of the FRG Ministry of Defense and therefore speaks with authority on European views. The context in which he cites the European commitment to MAD is that the SDI is widely seen as inimical to MAD. Of course, the language used in President Reagan's announcement of SDI left no doubt that he wished to find a better way to deter war than by means of the MAD doctrine. However, there are forms of strategic defense, ironically, that would enhance the ability of the United States to enforce the MAD doctrine. Furthermore, the official position of the United States is that MAD will not be given up until it is clear that another answer is feasible.

In my earlier companion study,[7] I confessed that I have always been perplexed about a doctrine that could depict strategic defense as the villain in the arms control drama for more than a generation. I derived some vindication in noting that Henry Kissinger recanted his earlier association with MAD and that the President made a dramatic appeal to break with this vengeful doctrine. Hoffman's point, that some Europeans felt comfortable that their guarantor was as vulnerable as they were, makes more sense to me than the guarantor deliberately wishing to remain vulnerable. There is a certain quality of human nature about this attitude, a case of "misery loving company." But I also made the pragmatic obser-

---

[6] Hubertus G. Hoffman, "A Missile Defense for Europe?," *Strategic Review*, Summer 1984.
[7] Davis, op. cit., p.15.

vation that the type of defense critically needed now, to defend military targets, is not in opposition to MAD. If we defend our ICBM forces, we can assure that enough of them will survive to be able to retaliate—which is the essence of MAD. In other words, we can restore the credibility of our present strategic doctrine before we give it up in favor of a more enlightened doctrine. Failing this, we are stuck with a long period when we cannot credibly enforce the present deterrence doctrine and cannot make the transition to a new one.

It must be understood that the restoration of the credibility of MAD, through the development of a hedge option to defend our retaliatory forces, is a prudent interim step and not an end to supplant the ultimate goals of SDI. As James Schlesinger has said, "the justification for strategic defense should never be based on assertions regarding the 'immorality' of deterrence. For the balance of our days the security of the Western world will continue to rest on deterrence. . . ."[8] I hope that the time will not be as distant as indicated by Dr. Schlesinger before SDI can fulfill its promise, but I agree that we cannot throw out MAD before SDI matures.

Marc Geneste, a French military analyst, has eloquently sounded a warning concerning the preservation of extended deterrence which has overtones of the Schlesinger admonition. While he attacks MAD as a discredited doctrine, and applauds the SDI movement toward a saner policy, he nevertheless warns of "dangerous strains in U.S. rhetoric" with respect to SDI. His central message is conveyed in the following quotation:

> . . . It is both regrettable and unalterable, however, that the only threat to America's survival—the atom—represents also the only viable shield of Europe against the Red Army divisions poised along the line of Europe's partition. . . . Yet, the current tendency in Washington, in connection with the public salesmanship of SDI, to speak indiscriminately of 'doing away with all nuclear weapons' carries grave dangers. . . .[9]

Decoupling

Werner Kaltefleiter, Professor of Political Science at Christian Albrechts University, Kiel, West Germany, has observed that the European concern about "decoupling" of the United States from Europe "seems to have become almost a conditioned reflex reaction to any U.S. strategic policy or program."[10] Nonetheless, the breadth of this reaction has touched even

---

[8] James R. Schlesinger, "SDI: The Quintessential Bargaining Chip," taken from a speech made at the 1984 National Security Issues Symposium, *Aerospace America*, July 1985.

[9] Marc Geneste, "Strategic Defense and the Shield of Europe," *Strategic Review*, Spring 1985.

[10] Werner Kaltefleiter, "Strategic Defense on the Broader Historical Stage," *Strategic Review*, Summer 1985.

current supporters of SDI and ATBM. Hubertus Hoffman records an early negative reaction to SDI in the Kohl government, and he cites an occasion in April 1984, during an interview following a meeting of the Nuclear Planning Group (NPG), when Minister of Defense Manfred Woerner declared himself to be clearly critical of the American plans for the development of an effective anti-missile defense. He quotes Dr. Woerner as seeing in the SDI plans the dangers of destabilization of the East-West balance, of a *decoupling* of the defense of Western Europe from that of the United States proper and "even of a splitting of the Western Alliance."[11]

Of course, Dr. Woerner now officially supports the SDI, as evidenced by his Memorandum of Agreement with the United States to cooperate in the program development. (It should be added that, while he supports SDI research, he seems to stop short of a philosophical commitment to the desirability of a transition from assured destruction to a defense-dominant doctrine.) He has also written the most definitive case in favor of ATBM of any European official.[12]

Thomas Enders has traced the evolution of Defense Minister Woerner's thinking on ATBM with considerable care in a recent study.[13] It is worth paraphrasing some of this account of Dr. Woerner's views, since they changed so dramatically over a two-year period, and because he is one of the most influential officials in the Alliance. Enders' chronology begins with an address by Dr. Woerner before the annual conference of the International Institute for Strategic Studies (IISS) on September 13, 1985. (It is perhaps noteworthy that Enders omits the earlier negative observations on SDI, cited above.) In that address Dr. Woerner pointed to the emerging Soviet capability to inflict a first-strike TBM attack with non-nuclear warheads and he identified the need to defend against both ballistic and nonballistic missiles. Significantly, he did not mention Soviet intermediate-range missiles. Enders portrays the Minister's position at this point as in neither the SDI nor the EDI camps, but rather as an independent force in shaping European policy to cope with an unfolding threat.

Enders later refers to Dr. Woerner's speech at the Eighth German-American Roundtable on NATO in December 1985, in which he further emphasized the Soviet short-range, nonnuclear tactical ballistic missile threat. At this point, the Minister introduced the label "extended air defense" as the umbrella term for defense against both cruise missiles and tactical

---

[11] Hoffman, op. cit., p.47. (Emphasis added.)

[12] Manfred Woerner, "A Missile Defense for NATO Europe," *Strategic Review*, Winter 1986.

[13] Thomas Enders, *Missile Defense as Part of an Extended NATO Air Defense* (Sankt Augustin bei Bonn: Konrad-Adenauer-Stiftung, May 1986).

ballistic missiles. This label, adopted by Enders in the title of his report, also connotes a continuum in the process of defending the air space over Western Europe, rather than a dramatic new initiative. In this speech, he spoke of cooperation with the SDI and dependence on this program to defend against Soviet intermediate-range ballistic missiles.

The most recent and definitive statement by Dr. Woerner on ATBM,[14] referred to briefly in Enders' study, contains a logically structured approach for responding to the Soviet short-range tactical ballistic missile threat. This article points out that defense against this threat might be accomplished through passive measures, destruction of Soviet missiles before their launch, and interception of the oncoming missiles before they reach their targets. The following guidelines were provided for an ATBM system: (1) The system must be nonnuclear. (2) The defense objective must be, in the first instance, a point-defense of priority targets on NATO territory. (3) The overall defense does not have to be impenetrable, nor does it have to cover all of Western Europe. (4) The system must have high survivability. (5) The system must be invulnerable to saturation.

The ABM Treaty

It was widely assumed that the ABM Treaty did not pertain at all to ATBM—until the most recent surge of interest in ATBM. This is still a defensible interpretation, based fundamentally on the fact that the treaty is concerned only with strategic defense of targets within the boundaries of the two signatories. However, a complex web of interpretations, gray areas, and questionable actions has been constructed recently by opponents of SDI and aficionados of the sport of hair-splitting. A reference point for the earlier interpretation is the 1983 Hoffman Study which identified an ATM intermediate option, noting, matter-of-factly, that "We can pursue such a program within the ABM Treaty constraints."[15] (The term "anti-tactical missile" was used by Hoffman and other analysts to include both ballistic missiles and air-supported vehicles in their threat.)

Extreme interpretations of the ABM Treaty abound in the literature, both by those who wish to use the treaty as a weapon against ATBM and by those who dignify such extremist ideas by embellishing them in articles. Hence, there are inferences such as, "The more effective an ATM is, the more it will look like an ABM, even if incapable of defense against SLBM and ICBM RVs. Ironically, therefore, the less effective the ATM, the easier

---

[14] Woerner, op. cit., p.17.

[15] Fred S. Hoffman, Study Director, *Ballistic Missile Defenses and U.S. National Security*, prepared for the Future Security Strategy Study, October 1983.

it might be to deploy in terms of public relations."[16] This curious insight poses a special problem to systems designers who, heretofore, were only interested in making systems effective; now they may have to be educated to make systems less effective in order to enhance the chances of their deployment. Another apparently serious notion was that the United States intends "to intercept Soviet strategic missiles attacking American territory, by ATBM systems deployed in Western Europe";[17] therefore, ATBM systems are banned by the treaty. It seems to make little difference that it is impossible for ATBM systems to have this kind of capability.

The extreme interpretations of ATBM treaty compliance issues cited above were taken from publications written by ATBM supporters who were characterizing the opposition. The more elaborate and convoluted arguments were contained in articles being published by organizations such as the Study Group on Peace Research and European Security (AFES) at the Institute of Political Science at Stuttgart University in the Federal Republic of Germany. This group finds support in U.S. anti-SDI organizations such as the National Campaign to Save the ABM Treaty and in other groups in Britain and France. In a barrage attack on ATBM (253 mostly negative references on defense in 71 pages), Hans Gunter Brauch, Director of AFES, presented every conceivable nuance of opposition to ATBM, with little selectivity or differentiation based on the quality of the arguments. Perhaps the most unambiguous statement in Brauch's publication is a quotation from a paper by Thomas K. Longstreth and John E. Pike, representing the U.S. group referred to above:

The unconstrained development and deployment of ATMs by both the U.S. and the U.S.S.R. threatens to circumvent both the letter and purpose of the ABM Treaty. The application of such systems to a strategic ABM role over the long term appears quite likely if the limits of their development and deployment are not clarified in the near future.[18]

Those who are attempting to stretch the ABM Treaty to prohibit ATBM, such as the authors of the above statement, usually use Articles VI and IX in their arguments. Article VI prohibits giving components other than ABM components—such as air defense radars and interceptors—a capability to counter *strategic* ballistic missiles. An integral part of this sanction against upgrading air defense components is the stipulation that they should not be tested in an ABM mode. At the time of the signing of the ABM Treaty, the SAM-D air defense system contained an ATBM require-

[16] David S. Yost, "Ballistic Missile Defense and the Atlantic Alliance," *International Security*, Fall 1982.

[17] Enders, op. cit., p.60.

[18] Hans Gunter Brauch, *Antitactical Missile Defense: Will the European Version of SDI Undermine the ABM Treaty?* (Stuttgart, FRG: Ag Friedensforschung und Europaische Sicherheitspolitik [AFES], Universitaet Stuttgart, July 1985).

ment, and this was not an issue. Later, Senator Symington and others raised questions about the relationship of the modest SAM-D tactical missile capability and the treaty, but this never became a serious question—the operative rule for compliance was to avoid testing the system in an ABM mode. Another provision of Article VI is that early warning radars should be deployed only along the periphery of each nation and oriented outward, a provision violated by the Soviets with their Krasnoyarsk radar.

Article IX prohibits the transfer of *ABM systems or their components* limited by the treaty to other states. Both of these articles clearly pertain to ABM and not ATBM and to defense against strategic missiles and not tactical missiles. They were intended to prevent a creeping violation of the treaty, to close loopholes which might be used to create a strategic defense capability outside the treaty limits, either in the territories of the two parties or by their allies. It requires an extended unilateral U.S. interpretation of these articles of the treaty, resulting in unverifiable system design restrictions, to conclude that it prohibits the development and deployment of ATBM systems.

If their "chapter and verse" recitations of treaty provisions fail to present a convincing case that ATBM is not allowable, the critics resort to a "teleological" interpretation which provides far more license. The AFES paper referenced above used this technique. It is reminiscent of the Warren Court interpretations of the U.S. Constitution. It was not what is literally contained in the Constitution, in a strict constructionist sense; it is what can be extrapolated by other criteria, such as "what is fair." Using a "teleological" interpretation of the treaty, the AFES paper finds sweeping violations by any movement of the Alliance toward an ATBM system.[19]

It is interesting to note that the same people who express anguish over the threat posed to the treaty by the ongoing Alliance studies of ATBM are less concerned about the existing Soviet ATBM system, the SA-X-12. This system is nearing deployment and it has an undeniable ATBM capability, probably extending to strategic missiles. The Soviets have apparently adhered to the rule to avoid testing this system against strategic missiles. Having followed this rule of the game, they clearly saw nothing in the treaty to stop them from going ahead with this system; curiously, there seems to be a quiet consensus in the United States and allied nations that the Soviets were right. It was right for them to build an ATBM system, but the rules must be more restrictive for the Western Alliance.

---

[19] Ibid., p.60.

Defense Makes Conventional Conflict More Likely

The fear that strategic defense would make conventional war more likely in NATO has been expressed in a number of different ways by European spokesmen. One formulation is that there are three possible outcomes to the East-West race to perfect strategic defenses, and two of them are bad for West European security. These outcomes are that either the United States or the Soviet Union will succeed in building effective defenses or both nations will. Obviously, it would not be desirable for the Soviet Union to have a unilateral advantage in strategic defense, in addition to its superiority in ICBMs and conventional weapons. While a U.S. advantage would be stabilizing, the prospect of both superpowers having ATBM defenses raises the specter of an increased threat of conventional war in Europe. One West German strategic analyst, in examining the situation where both sides possess comparable defenses, warned that "This is not an attractive scenario for Western Europe: it augurs a far-reaching neutralization of Western strategic and 'Eurostrategic' offensive systems, with the consequence that the conventional and tactical-nuclear superiority of the Warsaw Pact would become dominant in the 'correlation of forces' in Europe."[20]

A corollary to the fear that defense by both superpowers would increase the dangers of conventional war is the belief that President Reagan's suggestion to give the Soviets SDI technology is not a good idea. This idea has been criticized on other grounds, but to most Europeans it is not reassuring to think that the United States would hand the Soviets the means to defend themselves. This would be tantamount, in their view, to guaranteeing an increased emphasis on conventional means of conflict. Even if they too were defended, and all nuclear missiles were negated, the avenues of conventional warfare, where the Soviets have a preponderant advantage, would be opened wide.

These concerns that defense would make conventional warfare more likely, while legitimate, are based on a remote contingency, and the basis for them can be dispelled by allied action. In the first place, the time period when strategic defenses are likely to reach such a level of perfection that they "render nuclear weapons impotent and obsolete," and thereby may herald a renewed emphasis on conventional weapons, is many years away. As previously noted, we need to pay attention to the near term when defenses are needed to bridge the gap to a new doctrine, to defend our retaliatory forces, and to restore the credibility of deterrence and extended deterrence. During this period, defenses are clearly usable to extend the U.S. nuclear deterrent and to offset the Soviet advantages

---

[20] Kaltefleiter, op. cit., p.20.

in conventional forces. Beyond the near term, the portent of a nuclear standoff when conventional force structures favor the Warsaw Pact can be ameliorated by increasing Western conventional forces. General Bernard W. Rogers has said that we have "mortgaged our defense to the nuclear response," and must go ahead with "concerted modernization of NATO conventional forces that is within both the technological and economic reach of the member nations."[21] Whether General Rogers' plea to increase conventional strength in NATO is heeded or not, it is certainly consistent with any possible outcome of the new emphasis on strategic defense and ATBM. In the scenario where nuclear offensive weapons are neutralized by defense, it would be a sad fate indeed if our conventional inferiority placed us in a worse posture than when nuclear weapons were undeterred.

Defense Must Be Perfect

The argument that defense effectiveness must approach 100 percent can only be rationalized for the case of defending cities. Here the consequences of even one "leaker" are so great that a perfect defense is a reasonable goal. For the case of defense of military targets, some leakage can be tolerated and still satisfy militarily significant defense goals. The role of ATBM is usually viewed, at least initially, as defending critical military assets such as nuclear strike forces, air defense sites, and command headquarters. The defense of such critical military targets was analyzed in the SRS study, and it was concluded that these targets could be defended adequately with imperfect, state-of-the-art defense components. For most targets in the SRS data base for NATO, defense leakages on the order of 20 percent, representative of a single tier terminal defense system, could provide adequate levels of defense. There were some critical targets, however, where higher quality defense was desirable: an objective of 4 percent leakage was set for a few targets, representative of two tiers of defense, an exoatmospheric tier and a terminal, endoatmospheric tier.

Defense Raises Questions Concerning the INF Decision

The critics who have raised the INF issue anew, in connection with ATBM, appear to be returning to a dependably provocative issue to buttress their criticism. It is analogous to saying that the U.S. strategic modernization program is not needed now that SDI has been launched. There is scant logic to the argument that offensive forces can be eliminated or reduced

---

[21] General Bernard W. Rogers, USA, "Greater Flexibility for NATO's Flexible Response," *Strategic Review*, Spring 1983.

because SDI research has begun or that ATBM studies are underway. Defensive systems are needed, as previously stated, first and foremost to defend vulnerable military targets, including offensive forces, until a defense-dominant strategy can be implemented. The dual-track decision of December 1979, resulting in the upgrading of the INF in NATO, should not be modified in any way because of the inchoate ATBM plans. This decision represents a response to the Soviet SS-20 deployment already in place, and any delay in implementing the decision, ostensibly to await the arrival of ATBM, would be a move in the wrong direction for the wrong reason.

Defense Erodes Extended Deterrence and Flexible Response

The final two arguments against ATBM are closely coupled and equally invalid. Of course, extended deterrence is a part of flexible response; it is the ultimate rung in the escalation ladder envisioned in the flexible response doctrine. Both of these doctrines have been strengthened by U.S. strategic modernization and INF deployment programs, but they are still in need of repair. As previously noted, General Rogers has empha-sized the need to strengthen the first rung on the ladder, that of conven-tional force response. There are also the glaring twin problems of the vulnerability of the U.S. land-based ICBM force, the heart of extended deterrence, and the growing vulnerability of the INF forces and other NATO military assets to quantitatively superior Soviet INF and short-range ballistic missiles. It strains the imagination to see how either of these problems could be exacerbated by ATBM deployment; however, the charge has been made and it is instructive to probe the elusive reasons behind it.

One of the most revealing discussions in the aforementioned AFES paper is the one that clarifies the conflict, as seen by the AFES group, between ATBM and flexible response. It is not that ATBM weakens flexible response; on the contrary, that group implicitly concedes that ATBM strengthens flexible response. The opposition to ATBM stems from the very fact that it *does* protect the assets needed to implement the intermediate options embodied in flexible response and thereby assigns strategic nuclear forces to a more remote contingency role. Hans Brauch uses a quotation from Simon Lunn to explicate this view: "Europeans have tended to advocate a strategy of absolute deterrence through the immediate threat of all-out war, and have looked with suspicion and unease at any devel-opment that appears to distract from this ultimate threat. . . ."[22] Brauch goes on to portray this outlook as a conflict of interest with the Americans

---

[22] Brauch, op. cit., p.24.

by noting that the Americans are looking beyond deterrence, emphasizing the need to deter conflict at all possible levels, and, should deterrence fail, seeking to terminate the conflict short of all-out nuclear war. He contends that this basic conflict of interest has manifested itself in the debate on MLF and ABM in the 1960s, on TNF in the late 1970s and early 1980s, and on SDI most recently since 1984. He concludes that the "rather theological dispute" on coupling or decoupling has concealed this more fundamental issue from the public view.

If this rationale for opposing ATBM is accepted, there is little remaining room for constructive debate. That is to say, if the doctrine of flexible response, which has been the foundation of NATO since 1967, is repudiated, then the case for defending the forces that make the doctrine viable is academic. Why argue for ATBM if the objective is to revert to a doctrine of massive retaliation, a hair-trigger, singular response option with no intermediate steps? There is a perverse logical consistency to this position, even if it is appallingly anachronistic. Hopefully, the ultimate fate of ATBM will be decided on the basis of the conventional assumption that it is desirable to preserve flexible response.

David Yost confirms the existence of the above point of view, noting that many Europeans "prefer a concept of deterrence without intra-war escalation boundaries," and that "their faith in strategic deterrence is often associated with the assumption that more credible theater war-fighting capabilities would undermine strategic nuclear deterrence."[23] He goes on to construct a strategic rationale that argues against ATM—a rationale derived from the flexible response doctrine. This rationale is based on the assumption that the Soviets have the only ATM deployment, or that they have a more effective deployment; hence, the option within flexible response of what might be called "deliberate limited escalation" would be undermined. NATO's strike forces would have to be larger to produce the same effect. While this is true, the question is not the one implied: Would our deployment of an ATBM system trigger a like response on the part of the Soviets? The fact of the matter is that they are already deploying ATBM; the question is whether we would be better off by also deploying ATBM.

Manfred Woerner has expressed the threat to flexible response, and the role of allied ATBM in restoring its credibility, in clear and uncluttered terms:

The Soviet Union is thus attaining a qualitatively new capability for executing the "conventional fire-strike"—namely, the capability to destroy with conventionally armed missiles a

---

[23] Yost, op. cit., p.168.

large number of important military objectives in NATO territory. . . . By concentrating missile strikes on prime NATO targets over massively attacking Warsaw Pact air and ground formations, the Soviet Union could prevent, delay or obstruct numerous NATO response options in the critical initial phase of a conflict. . . . The only politically and strategically acceptable alternative for NATO, therefore, is a direct defense against Soviet missiles.[24]

Jacquelyn Davis and Robert Pfaltzgraff have thoroughly researched the spectrum of West European opinion on strategic defense, in the context of extended deterrence and flexible response, and they find that European critics have thus far failed to appreciate the factors that make comprehensive active defense a natural evolutionary course in NATO defense planning. "What such European critics of the strategic defense concept fail to realize is that, given the Soviet rejection of the assured destruction paradigm and in light of Moscow's advanced development of its own extensive strategic defense capabilities, the practical effect of a campaign to undermine the U.S. program will be to erode further NATO's strategy of flexible response."[25] They note that flexible response is an inherently defensive strategy and that it is broad enough to embody strategic defense. Indeed, they conclude that "the efficacy of deterrence based on flexible response will depend increasingly on technologies for defense from the battlefield to the strategic-nuclear level."

Defense as a Response to Imbalances

Much of the criticism of strategic defense and ATBM is based on the false premise that it would be an initiative that would upset the current balance and trigger an unwanted response on the part of the Soviets. *The real case for defense is as a response to Soviet actions which have created serious imbalances.* The following are the more portentous imbalances created by Soviet initiatives which are correctable by the deployment of defenses:

- The unmistakable Soviet counterforce capability against U.S. land-based ICBMs weakens deterrence and extended deterrence. It can be offset with active defense. It is not proposed that the United States unilaterally break out now from the ABM Treaty to defend the land-based ICBM force, but an advanced terminal defense system should be prototype-developed, on an accelerated schedule, so that a defense could be rapidly deployed in the event of a Soviet ABM breakout. In addition to preparing a hedge for defending U.S. ICBM forces, the advantages in near-term BMD capability currently enjoyed by the Sovi-

---

[24] Woerner, op. cit., p.15.

[25] Jacquelyn K. Davis and Robert L. Pfaltzgraff, Jr., *Strategic Defense and Extended Deterrence: A New Transatlantic Debate* (Cambridge, Mass.: Institute for Foreign Policy Analysis, National Security Paper No. 4, February 1986).

ets would be neutralized by a prototype development. These ominous Soviet actions—deployment of a massive ICBM counterforce capability and development of a BMD breakout potential—require a U.S. defensive reaction.

- The Soviet deployment of INF and short-range ballistic missiles threatens to take out NATO military targets in a preemptive strike, perhaps without resorting to the use of nuclear warheads, and there is no defense against them. This is a new threat, a unilateral action by the Soviets that profoundly changes the balance of power in NATO. It is an action to which we can respond logically by deploying an ATBM system. Such a system can be deployed within the terms of the ABM Treaty.

- The Soviets have developed an ATBM system, the SA-X-12, which will soon be deployed. It is an effective system which can degrade the effectiveness of the NATO-deployed Pershing I and II and Lance missiles. The Soviets were the first to develop an ATBM system. It has already been tested. It is a precedent under the ABM Treaty. Neither the United States nor the European allies have complained that the SA-X-12 violates the ABM Treaty. This is an action by the Soviets which can be countered by deployment of an allied ATBM system, not merely as a mirror-image, but to protect NATO offensive forces which will have to penetrate Soviet ATBM systems.

These unilateral destabilizing actions by the Soviets can be met by defenses which are technologically advanced, including the use of nonnuclear warheads. Therefore, the West should not be deterred from responding to these provocative actions for fear of increasing the inventory of nuclear warheads. It has been demonstrated that nonnuclear warheads are effective against ballistic missiles, first by the Homing Overlay Experiment (HOE) against exoatmospheric warheads in 1984, and then by the short-range HIT (or FLAG—flexible, lightweight, agile guidance) experiment against endoatmospheric warheads in 1986. These represent major technological milestones and remove much of the objectionable aspects of defenses.

4. The Threat and ATBM Options

The Threat

Figure 1 shows the modern Soviet tactical ballistic missiles (TBM) arrayed against some of the potential defense components which can be used to engage these missiles. These four tactical missiles (a fifth, an SLBM, is also included in the figure, since these missiles could be used against targets in NATO) constitute a very imposing threat to NATO assets; they can be accurately targeted against high-value aimpoints, and there is no current defense against them. As indicated at the top of Figure 1, these missiles have highly varied trajectories. The three shorter-range missile trajectories are shown at about two-thirds maximum range, and the SS-20 is shown at about one-third maximum range. The horizontal broken line and arrow denoting the exoatmospheric regime show that only the SS-20 spends a large part of its flight time above the atmosphere and is therefore confidently engageable by exoatmospheric BMD components.

The following summary of the characteristics of these tactical ballistic missiles is taken from the authoritative publication *Soviet Military Power*:[26]

The SS-21 is a division-level system that is replacing the older FROG-7. It has a range of about 120 kilometers compared to the FROG-7's range of about 70 kilometers, and is more accurate and reliable, thus enabling greater targeting flexibility and deeper strikes. Currently, there are some 500 FROG and SS-21 launchers opposite NATO.

The SS-23 is the replacement for Scud, normally deployed in brigades at army and front level. It has a range of 500 kilometers, versus the Scud's 300 kilometers, and improved accuracy. There are over 400 Scud launchers opposite European NATO, and these are expected to be replaced by SS-23s.

The SS-12 Scaleboard missile, with a range of about 900 kilometers, is expected to be replaced by the SS-22 of similar range but greater accuracy. (Figure 1 uses the label "SS-12 Mod 2" rather than SS-22, because of differences within the intelligence community over whether this is a replacement system or a Scaleboard upgrade.) Over 70 SS-22 launchers are opposite European NATO.

---

[26] Department of Defense, *Soviet Military Power, 1984* (Washington, D.C.: U.S. Government Printing Office, April 1984), and subsequent 1985 and 1986 editions.

FIGURE 1

THE TBM THREAT VS. CANDIDATE DEFENSE SYSTEMS

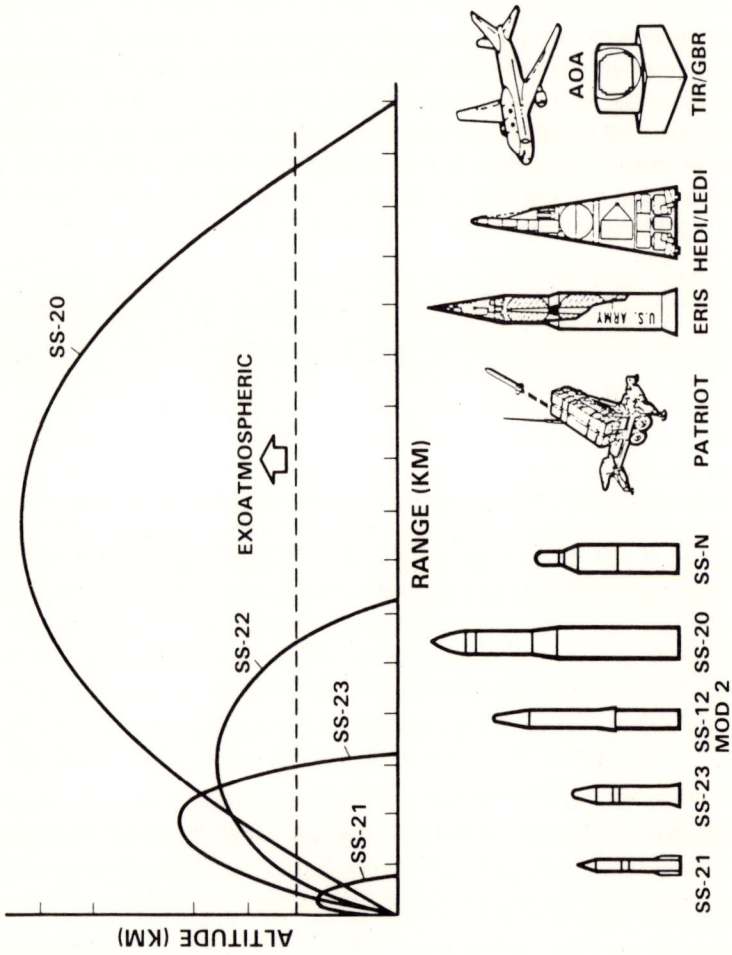

All three of the short-range ballistic missiles—the SS-21, -22, and -23—are capable of delivering nuclear, chemical, or conventional warheads.

Deployment of the SS-20 longer-range INF began in 1977. Each missile carries three MIRVed nuclear warheads. To date, about 400 SS-20s have been deployed, two-thirds of which are opposite NATO. The mobility of the SS-20 system enables both on- and off-road operation. As a result, the survivability of the SS-20 is greatly enhanced because detecting and targeting them is difficult when they are field deployed. In addition, the SS-20 launcher has the capability of being reloaded and refired; the Soviets stockpile refire missiles. The SS-20s also have very significant improvements in accuracy and reaction time over the older SS-4s and SS-5s. The Soviets are flight-testing an improved version of the SS-20, which is expected to be more accurate than its predecessor.

The critical parameter for short-range ballistic missiles that determines their efficacy for *nonnuclear* missions is accuracy. The reported improvements in the accuracy of the three Soviet short-range missiles has given rise to a new concern—notably, the previously-mentioned concern expressed by FRG Defense Minister Manfred Woerner—about the use of this class of missile against discrete military targets. At a recent meeting in Kiel, Germany, this subject was very controversial, and different participants presented a wide range of estimated CEPs (circular error probabilities)—a range that extends from effective counterforce utility to very limited utility.[27] One U.S. speaker at the meeting cited a CEP of a "few tens of meters" for these missiles, but others felt that Soviet technologies would not support an accuracy better than an order of magnitude greater than this. Thomas Enders cites U.S. sources for an estimate of 30 meters CEP for the SS-21 and SS-23 systems; but he points out that Uwe Nerlich feels that this estimate is greatly exaggerated, and he cites Stephen M. Meyer as the source of estimates of 100-200 meters for the SS-21 and 200-600 meters for the SS-23.[28]

Senator Dan Quayle, a member of the Senate Armed Services Committee, uses the low end of the spectrum of estimates of Soviet short-range missile accuracy in the following excerpt from a recent article:

Moreover, because these "shorter-range" missiles can potentially reach targets within ranges of up to 1000 kilometers—and by the 1990s are expected to command accuracies of *within 50 feet*—it is quite likely that, armed with chemical and improved conventional

---

[27] Institute for Foreign Policy Analysis, Inc., Cambridge, Mass.; Hermann Ehlers Foundation, Kiel, Gurlittstr, FRG; and Institute of Security Studies at the Christian-Albrechts-University, Kiel, FRG, "Strategic Defense and European Security: A Transatlantic Conference," June 19-21, 1986.

[28] Enders, op. cit., p.27.

warheads, they could destroy virtually all of NATO's key military assets that heretofore were assigned to nuclear warheads."[29]

Some of the characteristics of these tactical ballistic missiles make them more difficult to defend against than strategic missiles and some characteristics make them less difficult. On balance, they are not as technically stressing to defense systems as strategic missiles, but the need to make ATBM components mobile and to achieve a favorable cost-exchange ratio presents a great challenge to the defense system designer. The characteristics that tend to make this class of targets more difficult to engage than strategic missiles include: (1) the short times-of-flight (as short as 3-4 minutes) stress the reaction capability of the defense; (2) a wide range of velocities and reentry angles (a large V-gamma map), going from depressed to lofted and from very slow to strategic-class velocities; and (3) the difficult nonnuclear lethality problems associated with defending against conventional, chemical and nuclear warheads, particularly the chemicals. In the strategic case, the lethality problem is usually nuclear defensive warheads against nuclear offensive warheads, and the defense kill probabilities are relatively high.

Some of the tactical ballistic missile characteristics that make them less difficult for defense are: (1) many of these vehicles have relatively large signature characteristics, that is, radar cross-sections and emissivity areas, giving the defense plenty of signal for acquisition; (2) given the large number of targets in the "blue" data base relative to the projected number of TBM warheads available, the expected traffic density is not as great as for a highly MIRVed and penetration-aided strategic threat, and thus does not pose as great a saturation problem for the defense; and (3) sophisticated penetration aids are not as likely to be used for TBMs as for strategic missiles and, therefore, discrimination is not as difficult.

Damage Potential of the Threat

In the SRS study, and other ATBM studies, rigorous analysis of the damage potential of the ballistic missile threat to NATO assets has been carried out. This study concentrated on military assets, and it assigned values to a large number of aimpoints, grouped into six different categories of targets: nuclear strike forces (Pershing and GLCM targets), air defense sites (Patriot), nuclear storage sites, communication nodes, military forces, and logistical supply depots. The categories of targets were assigned different priorities which were varied to test sensitivities. The target value

---

[29] Senator Dan Quayle, "Beyond SALT: Arms Control Built Upon Defenses," *Strategic Review*, Summer 1986. (Emphasis added.)

and category priority system allowed the results of a TBM attack to be expressed in aggregate damage to the value structure.

The common approach for NATO ATBM studies is to perform a laydown of the TBMs on the value structure, using different scenarios for both "red" and "blue" preparation time. For example, a 0/1 scenario is defined as zero preparation time for the blue forces (a surprise attack) and one day of preparation by the red forces, and a 10/14 scenario is a "generated" case where both sides have longer periods of preparation. The computerized computations of damage to the blue data base are carried out for both undefended and defended cases in order to quantify the contributions of the defense. One pitfall of this type of analysis, which must be avoided in structuring the defenses, is that aggregate damage may be acceptable, but individual target classes are subject to excessive damage. For example, key command headquarters or communications nodes, which must survive to conduct a retaliatory strike, may be knocked out even though gross damage is held to an acceptable level.

In order to get a comprehensive picture of the threat to NATO, it is necessary to analyze both the air-supported threat and TBMs. Furthermore, it is necessary to treat the nonnuclear and nuclear attacks separately in order to measure the severity of different levels of escalation. It becomes very complex to treat all of these variables rigorously in attack models; typically, simplifying assumptions are made about the air-supported threat, such as overall percent attrition. The nonnuclear and nuclear damage levels have been estimated with reasonable accuracy, although the "damage" produced by chemical warheads defies accurate quantification and the kill probabilities of nonnuclear warheads, say against airfields, is time-sensitive and highly accuracy-dependent.

Studies indicate that if the TBM threat is restricted to nonnuclear warheads, the damage expectancy to NATO assets, in the aggregate, is not overwhelming. This is true even if very good accuracy is ascribed to the nonnuclear missiles; the results are driven by the fact that there are a large number of aimpoints, and nonnuclear warheads must be applied in profusion to take out the targets, especially extended targets such as airfields. The degree of concern expressed recently about Soviet nonnuclear TBMs, such as the above quotation of Senator Dan Quayle, seems inconsistent with this observation, but it is probably the improved utility of these missiles below the nuclear threshold that magnifies the concern. Without question, it is a significant new military capability to be able to apply accurate nonnuclear ballistic missiles in surgical strike missions against key targets.

It is the use of tactical ballistic missiles in a nuclear strike, despite the relative deemphasis of this scenario in recent public statements, that is devastating to NATO survival. Given the large number of nuclear warheads in the Soviet inventory (especially the SS-20s), their high kill probability, and the lack of any defense against them, their use against NATO targets reduces the survivability of key military assets to zero. In fact, there is a large overkill capability built into the Soviet inventory. This observation is based on the results of damage computations and has nothing to do with Soviet strategy and tactics. However, some analysts raise questions about the likelihood that the Soviets would depend so heavily on non-nuclear options and confer escalation control to NATO forces. Stephen J. Cimbala contends that "over the past several years, a growing number of Western analysts have begun to stress the possibility of the USSR developing a 'conventional-only' option for conflict in Europe, without due regard to its substantial capability for theater nuclear warfare."[30] He acknowledges that Soviet planners would prefer to avoid the risks entailed in using nuclear weapons, but he notes that there are "plausible reasons to question whether the USSR would rely on the probability of a quick and decisive victory in Europe without resort to nuclear arms," and that "Soviet theater capabilities for nuclear warfare are being improved, and new doctrinal and tactical concepts are as suited to nuclear as to conventional warfare."

What Threat Should an ATBM System be Designed to Counter?

Before addressing defense options for ATBM, it is necessary to consider the question of what tactical ballistic missiles the ATBM system should be designed to counter. The preoccupation noted above with short-range nonnuclear missiles, and the perplexing neglect of the SS-20 in recent official and unofficial statements, leads to the inference that nuclear and INF class systems should be disregarded in ATBM planning. This is exactly the opposite from the situation three to four years ago, when public statements and the literature were transfixed on the awesome threat of the SS-20 and the prospects of defending against it. As previously noted, the dual-track decision in 1979 provided a response to the SS-20 by deployment of upgraded INF forces by the Alliance, but this could scarcely be viewed as a reason to abandon all interest in defending against it.

With respect to the question of TBM nuclear versus nonnuclear warheads, much of the recent literature emphasizing the nonnuclear threat acknowl-

---

[30] Stephen J. Cimbala, "Soviet 'Blitzkrieg' in Europe: The Abiding Nuclear Dimension," *Strategic Review*, Summer 1986.

edges the obvious fact that a defense system cannot feasibly differentiate between the two types of warheads. Therefore, there is tacit assent to the notion that nuclear warheads are likely to be engaged by an ATBM system, even though they are not the primary targets the system should be designed to counter. There are a number of problems with this reasoning, not the least of which is that a defense designed against nonnuclear warheads will not have the required "keepout" capability against nuclear warheads. That is, a system designed against *nonnuclear* missiles can allow the missiles to come closer to the targets being defended before they are destroyed, with a resultant relaxation of component performance requirements, than a system designed against *nuclear* missiles. In effect, this means that an ATBM system must be designed to counter nuclear missiles in order to have a capability against both nuclear and nonnuclear missiles; the reverse approach will not work.

If the logic of designing against nuclear missiles is accepted, with the corresponding requirement of providing a safe keepout zone against nuclear effects, then the next question is where to cut off the range requirement. Should an ATBM system be effective only against the 120-kilometer SS-21? Should the range capability be extended to the 500-kilometer SS-23? The 900-kilometer SS-22? What about the 5000-kilometer SS-20? The first technical consideration to be noted about the relationship of ATBM capability to target range is that there is not a sharp boundary between having some capability and having none. Typically, the size of the defended area, or footprint, of a defense system decreases with increasing threat range, and the forward edge of the footprint moves in with increasing threat range. A crossover occurs when the footprint shrinks to a point or the forward edge recedes to the location of the battery, at which point only self-defense capability is enforced. Therefore, an ATBM system is usually designed to provide some level of desired coverage (footprint) against a design threat, and it will have less coverage against longer-range threats and more coverage against shorter-range threats.

It appears that concern over treaty issues has strongly influenced considerations of what TBM ranges a U.S. ATBM system should be designed to counter. Even the advertisement for the competitive Theater Defense Study from the Army's Strategic Defense Command excluded reference to the SS-20 INF-class missile and emphasized the short-range ballistic missiles. It is true that if a defense system is designed for a capability against the 5000-kilometer SS-20, it will have an inherent capability against strategic missiles, particularly SLBMs, and therefore be contentious under the ABM Treaty prohibition against giving a non-ABM system an ABM capability. However, it is technically impractical to affix rigidly a cut-off range for an ATBM system that will assure no capability against strategic missiles. The Soviets did not do this with their SA-X-12 system, and there have been no serious allegations of a treaty violation. The only practical and verifiable rule is to avoid "testing in an ABM mode," a rule apparently followed by the Soviets and one that the West could follow without serious design compromise.

The worst thing that could happen, as the "ATBM surge" begins to take shape, is that political restraint will override tactical requirements in designing the system(s). If the SS-20 threat is excluded from ATBM design requirements, or even if this threat is reserved for "eventual" solution by the SDI program, then the most menacing element of the TBM threat will be left unanswered for an indefinite period of time. The critical targets in NATO, including the independent deterrent forces of Britain and France, will remain hostage to this large nuclear force. This would be all the more unfortunate because the technology exists to blunt this threat. It is not beyond the state-of-the-art for active defense; in fact, it is a less stressing threat in many ways than the strategic threat. It appears that the greatest deterrent to an effective program to meet this threat is unilateral restraint based on an unduly restrictive interpretation of the ABM Treaty.

Building arbitrarily constrained ATBM defenses is analogous to building an inadequate fence around one's back yard. Suppose the objective is to keep the dogs out of the back yard and a fence only eighteen inches high is erected. It would be effective in keeping out terriers, Chihuahuas, and small poodles, but it would not stop Doberman pinschers and German shepherds. Not only would the effectiveness criterion be questionable, but the economics would not be sound since a four-foot fence could be built for only a slightly greater investment. It would be even more lamentable if the inadequate fence were erected in the mistaken belief that a local ordinance forbade building fences over eighteen inches high.

A more serious problem is that the SS-20 represents the majority of the warheads arrayed against Western Europe, their only purpose is to threaten Western Europe, and it is not prudent to entrust Alliance security to Soviet restraint in their use. Therefore, an investment in ATBM would not be a good bargain if it stopped short of countering this element of the threat. An ATBM system that is effective only against the nonnuclear short-range ballistic missiles could result in denial of a conventional attack option while making a devastating nuclear attack even more likely.

The prudent approach to ATBM, then, is to plan to counter all four TBMs. It may be that a combination of systems, such as air defense upgrades for the lower end of the spectrum and a dedicated system for the longer-range threat is the best approach for complete defense. Effectiveness against the longer-range SS-20 unavoidably connotes a capability against SLBMs; however, testing against SLBMs should not be conducted so that verifiable treaty provisions are observed.

ATBM Options

The defense components shown on the lower right part of Figure 1 suggest a range of options for defending against tactical ballistic missiles. The labels on these components are not meant to imply that these particular SDI and air defense elements are exclusively applicable to ATBM without modification. Rather, they are meant to convey that these generic types of components are candidates for ATBM. In general, the Patriot system, shown as the left symbol, is underdesigned for ATBM, and the four SDI components, shown by the four symbols on the right, are overdesigned for ATBM. In two cases, the LEDI interceptor and the GBR radar, the components are not currently in development and they could therefore be tailored for the ATBM mission.

The SDI components depicted as candidates for ATBM are basically terminal and late-midcourse components being developed in the Army part of the SDI program. Because of the nature of the TBM threat, these components have the greatest relevance for the ATBM mission. As previously noted, the most important factor in the selection of defense elements and operating regimes is the TBM trajectory. Unlike strategic ballistic missiles, which typically coast above the atmosphere for periods of over twenty minutes, tactical ballistic missiles have much shorter times-of-flight and they do not travel above the atmosphere for long periods of time. Therefore, space-based sensors and weapons, which are being vigorously pursued in the SDI program, normally cannot achieve long enough observation times to be effective. The SS-20 is an exception in that its longer trajectory results in sufficient time for exoatmospheric engagement.

The above discussion of space-based sensors and weapons for ATBM emphasizes the short time above the atmosphere available for observation and kill. It is possible that engagements within the atmosphere with certain types of space-based weapons will prove to be feasible. For precommit tracking within the atmosphere, the boost-phase plume tracking mode, used for strategic missile tracking, would be of limited use for TBMs because of their short boost period; however, other types of space-based sensors, such as radars, may provide sufficient precommit tracking. With respect to target kill, x-ray and neutral particle beam devices would not be useful within the atmosphere because of propagation limitations, but free-electron lasers and other kill devices may penetrate into the atmosphere effectively. Overall, it does not appear that the space-based elements being developed in SDI lend themselves naturally to the ATBM mission. It would seem to be reasonable to consider this class of weapon to be of secondary utility for ATBM, when and if it is deployed for strategic defense, rather than a class that is developed expressly for ATBM.

The current thinking about conventional approaches for ATBM can be generally partitioned into three categories of systems. One is the use of air defense upgrades, which seems to dominate West European thinking. Another category is adaptation of strategic defense systems, such as the SDI components shown in Figure 1. Finally, there is the category of dedicated ATBM systems, the approach of designing a system expressly for engaging TBMs. Experience suggests that the first category, upgrading of air defense systems, is limited to relatively short-range missiles such as the SS-21 and SS-23. Trying to stretch air defense systems much above this class of TBM results in extensive modifications which begin to raise the question of whether a new system would not be more cost-effective. As previously noted, the use of SDI components results in an overkill capability, and their use also raises treaty issues. It appears to be preferable to design a dedicated ATBM system that covers as much of the spectrum of TBMs as feasible, concentrating on the longer-range missiles.

The utility of the SDI components shown in Figure 1 will be discussed in the next section. Patriot will not be treated further, although that system is currently being modified to incorporate a limited, self-defense capability against the lower end of the TBM spectrum. It will not have a significant capability to protect other targets in NATO; however, there are more extensive modifications under consideration that may provide Patriot with this capability.

Utility of SDI Components for ATBM

The functions that defense components are required to perform are commonly classified as precommit and postcommit, with reference to the point when an interceptor is committed, or launched. The precommit functions include acquisition, discrimination, and tracking, and they depend primarily on the sensors (radar or optical) of the system. The postcommit functions include guidance and control of the interceptor, warhead fuzing, target kill, and kill assessment. The postcommit functions revolve around the interceptor and, depending on the type of guidance employed, some degree of interaction between the ground-based components and the in-flight interceptor. In Figure 1, three precommit sensors—AOA, TIR, and

GBR—and three interceptors—ERIS, HEDI, and LEDI—are illustrated. The utility and derivatives of these components will be briefly discussed.[31]

The ERIS interceptor and AOA precommit sensor operate together for late-midcourse exoatmospheric intercepts. The ERIS interceptor uses passive LWIR (long wavelength infrared) guidance. Its technology is traceable to the Homing Overlay Experiment (HOE), which successfully intercepted an ICBM warhead with a nonnuclear warhead in June 1984; therefore, its feasibility to perform exoatmospheric nonnuclear kill is not of high technical risk. ERIS is also traceable to the Defense Technology Study Team (Fletcher Panel) findings, a high-level panel convened to formulate technology plans following the President's announcement of SDI on March 23, 1983. The Fletcher Panel called for a cheap, dumb interceptor for late-midcourse intercepts—that is, an interceptor that does not require a great deal of costly on-board intelligence or maneuver capability. In response to this requirement, ERIS is designed to be placed into a small "error basket," and for minimal size and weight. It is designated by the AOA sensor; an alternate mode is for designation by the SSTS (space surveillance and tracking system) space-based system.

The AOA also uses passive LWIR optical sensors for acquisition, tracking, and discrimination. The sensors are mounted on an airborne platform which may be either a manned airplane (which is being used for the development program) or an RPV (remotely piloted vehicle) for tactical application. In addition to the difficult problem of discrimination, there is a stringent requirement for the AOA to perform accurate enough tracking on the target to place the ERIS into a very small "error basket" to achieve a lethal intercept. It appears that it will be necessary to correlate between two AOAs or to add active laser track to get the error volume down in the small tracking time available. As previously mentioned, the AOA and ERIS components would be good only against the SS-20 because it is the only TBM that is above the atmosphere long enough to be engaged. However, they provide a good margin of capability against the SS-20 (shoot-evaluate-shoot capability against many trajectories) and the ERIS provides a low cost-per-intercept solution.

The HEDI and TIR are a matched pair of components for high endoatmospheric operation. (These components are not independent of the exoatmospheric components; the latter hand over to the former in the standard mode of operation.) HEDI uses passive optics guidance to achieve intercepts at the upper reaches of the atmosphere. It has a minimum intercept altitude that would allow underflights by some TBMs. The TIR has a long-range acquisition capability in order to support the high-altitude mode of operation of HEDI. Because of the long-range and high-altitude operation of TIR, it cannot use discrimination based on atmospheric slowdown, the classic technique developed in earlier BMD programs. Instead, TIR must use body dynamics and imaging techniques for discrimination. Because of the extended reach of both HEDI and TIR, they are relatively large and they are not road mobile. These components have an overkill capability for the ATBM mission, embodying a degree of sophistication for discrimination and a level of resources that result in excessive size for optimal ATBM design. The most challenging requirement for high endoatmospheric operation, using components such as HEDI/TIR, is the achievement of nonnuclear kill. It is more difficult to achieve nonnuclear kill in the atmosphere than above the atmosphere, where ERIS operates.

As pointed out in the previous section, the low endoatmospheric components, LEDI and GBR, are not currently under development. They have been treated parametrically in studies, and they can be designed to be capable against the full range of TBMs. As with the high endoatmospheric components, nonnuclear kill is the most stressing development objective for these components. The most promising guidance modes for LEDI, for low-altitude nonnuclear kill, are active or semi-active radar homing. The technology for active homing guidance, using millimeter wave seekers, is under development by the Army Strategic Defense Command. Recently, this guidance mechanization was successfully demonstrated in the FLAG experiment, formerly referred to as the Short-Range HIT program. A high-velocity reentry body was intercepted and killed in an experiment at White Sands Missile Range using a millimeter wave active homing seeker. It is worth recalling that a semi-active homing mode was used over twenty-five years ago (as recounted in Chapter I) to achieve a nonnuclear kill of an Honest John target. While semi-active guidance is still a competitive technique, acting homing has certain advantages (e.g., fuzing and relative autonomy of the interceptor); another option which may hold promise is the combination of the two modes, forming a hybrid guidance scheme.

It is axiomatic that if nonnuclear kill is required of an ATBM system, then very accurate guidance and small miss distances are required, and this in turn leads to the selection of some form of homing guidance. The three basic forms of homing guidance (discussed above) are passive, active, and semi-active, operating in four different parts of the electromagnetic spectrum (LWIR, SWIR, microwave, and millimeter wave). It is conceivable that some guidance mode other than homing could prove to be feasible, perhaps a beam-rider, or that directed-energy weapons could be used in a later timeframe to effect nonnuclear kill. However, the conventional, low-risk approach to nonnuclear ATBM operation is homing guidance, and for mobile components, operating at low altitude, the preferred approach is millimeter active homing.

5. A Proposed Approach to ATBM

Multiple Mission Development

In my recent study, *Asymmetries in U.S. and Soviet Strategic Defense Programs*, I urged greater emphasis in the current U.S. program on near-term development and advocated the accelerated development of an advanced terminal defense system prototype, capable of both ATBM and defense of hardened military targets in the Continental United States. A mobile terminal defense system can be developed which can perform both missions effectively and thus provide economies in the development investment required. (At the present time, it does not appear that an RDT&E budget for separate systems for the two missions could win approval, but it should be possible to build a constituency for a single system that will satisfy these two critical missions.) The system could be deployed for the ATBM mission within the terms of the ABM Treaty, and it could serve as a rapidly deployable hedge option for the CONUS hardsite mission. To assure compliance with Article VI of the treaty, the system should be tested against Pershing and Lance targets, but not against strategic missile targets. It would not be necessary to make an ATBM deployment decision before embarking on a development program; the important initial decision is to develop a complete, integrated prototype system so as to minimize deployment leadtime.

The development of such a versatile terminal defense system would respond to all three of the destabilizing Soviet initiatives discussed earlier: the deployment of a counterforce capability to destroy the U.S. ICBM leg of the strategic triad, the deployment of tactical ballistic missiles capable of inflicting incapacitating damage to NATO military assets, and the deployment of an ATBM system to defend against NATO tactical ballistic missiles. The U.S. defense system would be a direct, deployable response to the Soviet SA-X-12 ATBM system and their TBM threat to NATO targets. In this role, it would be capable of restoring the credibility of flexible response. The system could be adapted to the role of defense of the U.S. ICBM forces, deployable in a short period of time in the event of a crisis, and thus provide a means of strengthening deterrence and extended deterrence.

At the aforementioned meeting in Kiel, Germany, in June 1986, I suggested that the U.S. official declaratory position on the inherent strategic missile capability of a terminal ATBM system should be as silent as the

Soviets have been on the SA-X-12. I was attacked by one American participant with a patriotic speech denouncing the practice of deceiving the American public on military capabilities. He apparently did not respect the right of states, or the U.S. government, to remain silent on imputed military capabilities. Whether this aversion extends to such sensitive military issues as stealth technology, where there is widespread suspicion of "deceiving the American public," is unknown, but it is a common and relatively benign official practice to "neither confirm nor deny" an imputed capability. Again, the key point with respect to the issue at hand is to avoid testing in an ABM mode.

I first became attracted to the idea of a multi-mission, ATBM-hardsite system when the findings of different studies came in with largely overlapping requirements for the components. For example, the SRS study concluded that a terminal ATBM radar average power should be about 20 percent higher than the LoAD/Sentry (optimized for hardsite defense) and the interceptor velocity should be about 20 percent lower. Since these two parameters can be traded off within a wide range, it became obvious that one set of components could satisfy both missions. In addition, it is highly desirable to make the radar mobile for both missions, indicating that the power-aperture product and total size of the radar should be approximately the same for both missions.

The comparison mentioned above further underscores the futility of drawing a line between tactical and strategic missile capability. Earlier it was explained that the footprint sensitivity with regard to missile range was not great, and that a system capable of defending against the SS-20 would have a built-in capability against strategic missiles. The above comparison reveals that the radar designed for defense against strategic missiles is *actually smaller than one designed for tactical missiles*, and the interceptor is only 20 percent faster. This is true because the targets being defended in the strategic case, ICBM silos, are harder (to nuclear effects) than in the tactical case, including such targets as airfields, and the consequent requirements of commit altitude, keepout region, and component performance are relaxed. Therefore, it is technically impossible to observe the treaty admonition not to "give" a non-ABM system an ABM capability in terms of the design features of a dedicated ATBM system. If an ATBM system is given a capability against the full range of TBMs, its design requirements may even exceed those of a strategic defense system. It is even questionable that this problem can be avoided by ignoring the SS-20 (as already noted, an extremely dangerous truncation of the threat); a terminal system fully capable against the 900-kilometer range SS-22, if some margin of capability is built in for electronic countermeasures (ECM) and other degrading factors, may "reach-up" to the SLBM threat.

If the extreme interpretation of Article VI of the treaty prevails, to the extent that the capability of an ATBM system must be arbitrarily held below that required to counter longer-range TBMs, then it may develop that a dual mission capability is not feasible. Furthermore, it may turn out that the economic justification for developing such a system at all will not stand up.

A Strawman ATBM System

Figure 2 illustrates a terminal defense system that would be capable against the full range of TBMs and adaptable to the defense of hardened military targets in CONUS (several key characteristics have been left blank to keep this illustration unclassified). It is generically related to the LoAD/Sentry system, for which several hundred million dollars of relevant R&D was carried out. For continuity with the SDI nomenclature, the radar and the nonnuclear interceptor depicted may be thought of as the GBR and LEDI components. The technology embodied in this system is highly advanced, including distributed data processing, high levels of integration and speed in microelectronics components, and active millimeter wave seekers for nonnuclear kill capability. The use of advanced technology will not preclude early system availability, since all of it is within reach in the next five years. An IOC by the mid-1990s is achievable.

The radar operates at a high microwave frequency band. Its design is distilled from a number of "paper" radars from various system studies as well as a few hardware development programs. The frequency selection was based primarily on relative resistance to ECM, high bandwidth, and adaptability to road mobility. In addition, the frequency band selected corresponds to a plentiful data base from intelligence radars that is relevant to all defense functions required, including the critical functions of bulk filtering and discrimination.

A dual mode interceptor is proposed which can operate in an active homing mode and a command guidance mode. The command guidance mode will be similar to prior terminal guidance schemes but somewhat more precise than the guidance mode designed for LoAD/Sentry. The active homing mode will be based on the recently demonstrated FLAG technology, with substantial improvement in the seeker performance. An improvement in seeker sensitivity of 19 db is required over the seeker now flying at White Sands Missile Range in order to meet tactical ATBM requirements.

FIGURE 2

EARLY TERMINAL SYSTEM CHARACTERISTICS

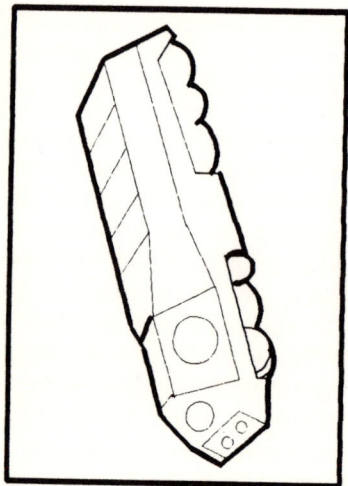

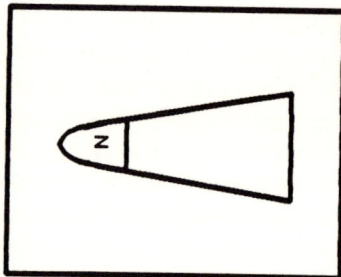

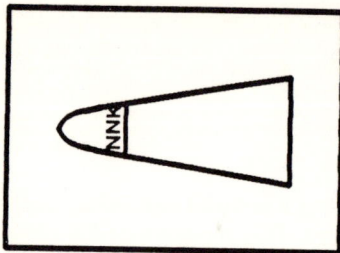

RADAR CHARACTERISTICS

FREQ: 10 GHZ
ELEMENTS, K: 12/4/4
PK PWR, KW:
AVE PWR, KW:
APERTURE: 6–8'

DATA PROCESSOR

DISTRIBUTED
2 MIPS PER NODE
7 NODES ON LINE, ONE SPARE

CONUS INTERCEPTOR

BURNOUT VEL:
LENGTH: 20'
BASE DIA: 54"
WT: 6 KLB
BURN TIME: 1.5 SEC
GUIDANCE: RADAR COMMAND

ATBM INTERCEPTOR

SAME
SAME
SAME
SAME
SAME
GUIDANCE: SEMIACTIVE OR
ACTIVE RADAR

40

The dual mode interceptor approach is proposed to satisfy ATBM requirements with a homing, nonnuclear system and to provide the option of using a command-guided nuclear system for hardsite defense. The maximum interceptor velocity was set by the radome limitations for the homing guidance mode. This velocity, as previously noted, is 20 percent lower than LoAD/Sentry and it is therefore slightly below optimum for the hardsite role; however, the radar power is higher than that provided for LoAD/Sentry and thus more than offsets the slower interceptor and results in a reasonable compromise for both roles.

The approach adopted for sizing the radar was what has been crudely called the "truck stuffer" concept. This means that the objective was the maximum power-aperture product that could be achieved while still retaining road mobility. It is clear that the resultant mobile radar design will be well suited for the CONUS hardsite application, but it may be somewhat unwieldy for theater operation. Further refinement of the design parameters is in order to optimize the design, but it is well within the trade-off space to meet both requirements with one system. One area of further investigation that should prove fruitful is radar resource allocation for search. For the low commit altitude and small azimuth coverage required for hardsite defense, a relatively modest surveillance zone is required. For the higher commit altitude and wider azimuth coverage required for ATBM, a more extensive surveillance zone is required. Interesting work has been done by some radar designers recently to net radars for the ATBM mission to conserve radar energy and support high commit altitudes. It appears at this point that two different software packages may be required in order to optimize radar search and other defense functions for each mission.

For both roles for the terminal defense system, plans should be made from the outset of development to integrate the system later with other tiers of SDI. In particular, the coupling between the terminal system and a late-midcourse (ERIS/AOA) overlay should be thought through in advance. For some ATBM defense objectives, it will be desirable to deploy a two-tier layered defense system (this would be in a breakout mode if SDI components are used, beyond the limits of the ABM Treaty). The low leakage provided by such a layered system is needed for very high priority targets, such as command headquarters. In addition, the large coverage of a late-midcourse system is attractive from a cost point of view and, particularly, for engagement of the SS-20. It should be remembered that the SS-20 is the only TBM that can be engaged by the exoatmospheric overlay, but it is the ideal solution for that missile. In CONUS, the proposed terminal system could serve as the bottom rung in a "full-up" SDI architecture; considered in an evolutionary context, it could be used effectively for intermediate missions, such as SAC base defense, with the late-midcourse tier.

Typical ATBM Effectiveness

Figure 3 shows the form of effectiveness results coming out of recent studies, which reveals a substantial capability against the four TBMs using defense components similar to the strawman terminal system described above and an exoatmospheric overlay representative of ERIS/AOA performance. The large, egg-shaped footprint at the bottom of this figure is for an exoatmospheric system against the SS-20 on a 2000-kilometer trajectory. A shoot-evaluate-shoot (SES) capability is achievable in this case; that is, an ERIS interceptor can be fired at an SS-20 warhead and, if it misses, another interceptor can be fired at the same warhead. In addition to the SES capability, economical coverage is obtained with the exoatmospheric system—only five or six AOAs would be required to cover all of Western Europe. Shown as an underlay are the smaller footprints of the terminal system. The diameter of these smaller footprints is about 1/10 the long dimension of the exoatmospheric footprint. The blow-up shows the geometry of the terminal footprints against the four TBMs. The type of terminal interceptor used for these footprints provided about the same area coverage for all four TBMs, but the leading edge of the footprints moved in toward the location of the defense (indicated by the crossed lines) as the range and velocity of the TBMs increased.

The drawdown curves shown at the upper left part of Figure 3 plot percent-survival of the total NATO military value structure versus the number of arriving TBM warheads for a nuclear attack. The "no defense" curve verifies the observation made earlier that a nuclear TBM attack against NATO would be disastrous. The situation is even worse than indicated by this curve, in that more recent estimates show that survivability can be drawn down to zero with less than 100 percent of the available TBM warheads. The curves marked with percentages at the top of the graph refer to leakage values (20, 10, and 4 percent leakage). The 20 percent figure corresponds to the leakage that could be expected of a terminal single tier defense and shows that such a deployment could restore survivability to an arbitrary goal of 70 percent. Higher survivability levels require lower leakage; the 4 percent curve, representative of a two-layer deployment, provides a very high level of protection of NATO assets. The only caveat that should be applied to this impressive picture of defense effectiveness is that it assumes that high kill probabilities are achievable with nonnuclear intercepts. While recent endoatmospheric nonnuclear demonstrations are encouraging, considerable R&D remains before this capability can be considered confidently available.

TYPICAL ATBM EFFECTIVENESS

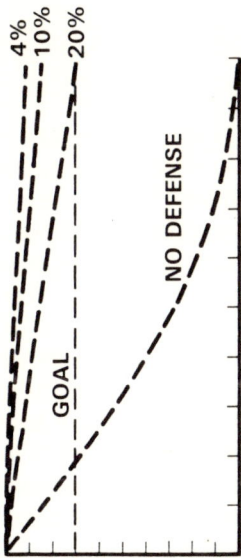

SS-23

SS-22

SS-20

SS-21

TERMINAL FOOTPRINTS

EXO SES FOOTPRINT
W/TERMINAL UNDERLAY

4%

10%

20%

GOAL

NO DEFENSE

DRAWDOWN - % SURV. VS. NO. WHS

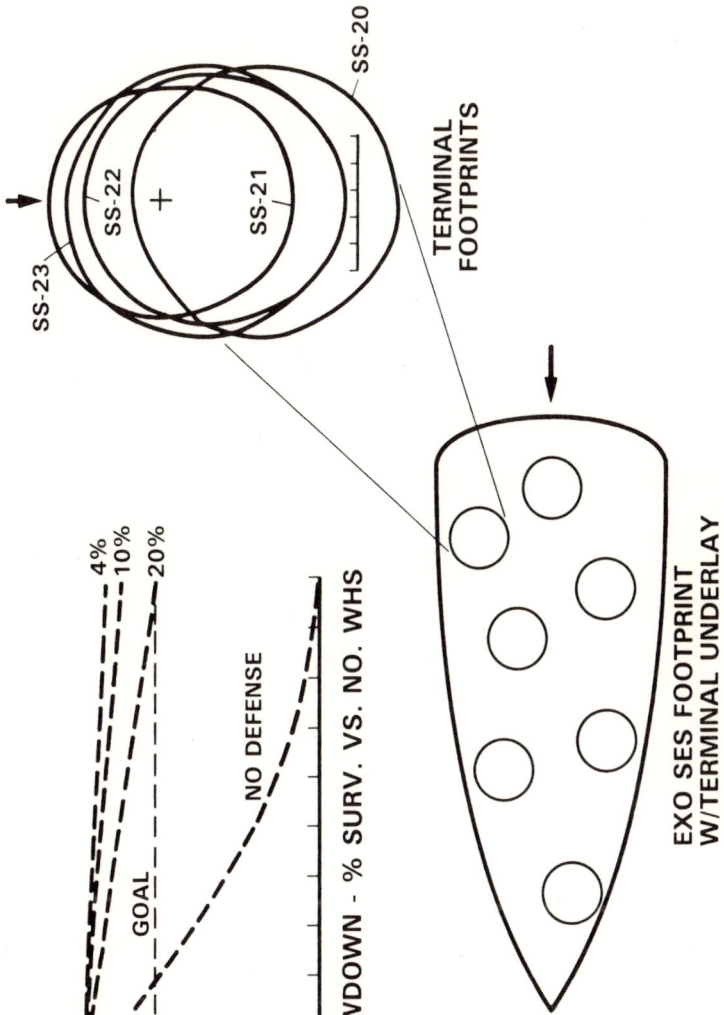

43

A Graduated ATBM Deployment Approach

A prudent approach to defense against the rapidly proliferating TBM threat is to deploy a limited system (or systems) as rapidly as possible, and then plan on "growing" the system to achieve more complete coverage and a higher quality of defense. The terminal system proposed here, perhaps combined with upgraded air defense systems—utilizing, for example, an improved Patriot capability—could be developed on an accelerated schedule to reach a deployment status by the mid-1990s. It could initially defend high priority targets and restore deterrence against the TBM threat for which there is no present defense.

Figure 4 emphasizes the limitation of terminal defense systems, also apparent from the footprints of Figure 3, in protecting large geographical areas: it requires a large number of modules, at considerable cost, to cover a large area. The graphs shown at the top of Figure 4 suggest the solution to this problem, in keeping with the concept of a graduated deployment. The plot of "radar power" versus "defense module coverage" shows the correct trends (without using classified numbers) for "slow" and "hot" (high acceleration and velocity) interceptors. This plot can be used to illustrate that the same module coverage can be obtained with a powerful radar and slow interceptor as with a weak radar and hot interceptor. The dotted lines illustrate the design point selected for the terminal system described above, which maximizes coverage while preserving mobility. The plot on the upper right, "number of modules" versus "defense module coverage," can be entered to obtain the number of modules required to cover a desired fraction of the value structure for a particular module coverage. The dotted lines on this plot illustrate that coverage of one-half of the value structure can be obtained for a relatively modest number of modules.

One way of characterizing the approach suggested above is that it minimizes the initial deployment of point defenses while planning on more economical area coverage later. As noted in the middle of Figure 4, the initial terminal defense deployment should be for the highest priority targets (perhaps nuclear strike forces, command headquarters, airfields, and air defense batteries), combined with counterbattery tactics and passive measures such as dispersal, hardening, concealment, and deception. With respect to the first passive technique, there would be significant synergism between active defense and dispersal in that the defense umbrella would allow additional time to disperse in the event of a surprise attack. Following the initial deployment, a number of "growth" paths would be available, some of which are illustrated.

44

FIGURE 4

PROBLEM: IT TAKES A LOT OF TERMINAL MODULES TO COVER ALL TARGETS

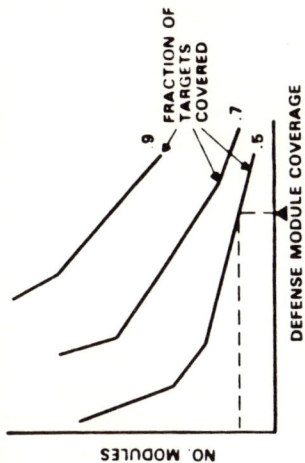

SOLUTION: INITIALLY DEPLOY TO DEFEND ONLY HIGHEST PRIORITY TARGETS, COMBINED WITH COUNTERBATTERY & PASSIVE

THEN GROW:

- **HANDOVER**

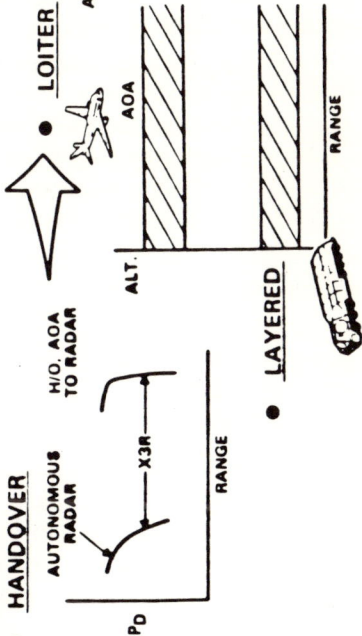

- **LOITER**

- **LAYERED**

45

The handover mode illustrated at the lower left of Figure 4 is a powerful intermediate option, exercisable short of a commitment to deploy a full exoatmospheric, area defense system. By the simple expedient of handing over from an optical adjunct, which may be deployable under the terms of the treaty, to the ground-based radar, the detection range of the radar can be increased by a factor of three. This enhanced capability may be used in a number of ways: the fraction of the value structure covered can be increased without increasing the number of modules; the effects of an increase in the ECM environment can be offset; or the degradation effected by reduced radar cross-section of the threat can be offset by handover.

The loiter mode illustrated in Figure 4 may prove to require interceptor modifications which are excessively complex or costly; however, some of the same increases in footprint size may be realized by remote deployment of interceptor farms. The ultimate defense for ATBM is probably the layered configuration illustrated, as previously described. Not only is the coverage increased by the addition of an exoatmospheric overlay, but the leakage is reduced, thus improving the quality of the defense. Again, the overlay system envisioned here is effective only against the SS-20; hence, the large coverage and low leakage of layered defense applies only to this missile. It would be desirable to formulate a concept, perhaps using higher altitude radar surveillance, and a HEDI-type interceptor operation, which provides an overlay against the shorter-range TBMs.

The Need for Immediate Prototype Hardware Development

The time is ripe to embark on a prototype hardware development program for ATBM. There is no need to wait for two or three years for all of the studies to be completed. The essential outlines of the system(s) needed are discernible, the technology is within grasp, and the urgency of the threat makes further delay extremely risky. The reason why an integrated system prototype development approach is required is that it is the only way, short of full-scale engineering development, that deployment lead-time can be reduced one year for every year of development. It represents the shortest path to a deployable system.

The "Quayle Amendment," introduced into the FY 1987 Senate Authorization Bill for SDI, and subsequently endorsed in the House of Representatives, stipulates that $50 million of the SDI budget should be set aside for application to ATBM. It calls for allied participation and matching funding for this mission. This U.S. Congressional action, which survived the authorization and appropriations process, and is included in the FY 1987 budget, supports the initiation of a serious ATBM development program. This level of funding would permit completion of concept definition in FY 1987, along with the development and demonstration of critical technologies, preparatory to the start of prototype system development in FY 1988. This would support an ATBM IOC in the mid-1990s, under an accelerated development schedule.

There are many observers, both for and against strategic defense, who are skeptical that any dedicated ATBM system can be developed before the year 2000. They contend that the most that can be done for the TBM threat is to upgrade air defense systems. This is an understandable position, since there are no recent precedents for developing and deploying a new weapon system in a short period of time. However, it is possible to lay out a schedule for a terminal system, such as the one described above, building on the experience of LoAD/Sentry and other BMD developments, which can credibly reach a mid-1990s availability. Every phase and program milestone can be scheduled without excessive concurrency, and with reasonable provisions for contingencies, if the budget is made available. It will require a multi-year budget commitment that will reach relatively large peaks, probably not absorbable in the current SDI outyear budgets, if the schedule is to be maintained. Furthermore, it will require streamlining of the procurement procedures and some shielding of the program from the vagaries of shifting political winds. But it can be done.

Glossary of Acronyms

AADS-70	advanced air defense system
AGARD	NATO's Advisory Group for Aerospace Research and Development
AOA	airborne optical adjunct
ATM	anti-tactical missile
ATBM	anti-tactical ballistic missile
CEP	circular error probability
CONUS	Continental United States
ECM	electronic countermeasures
EDI	European Defense Initiative
ERIS	exoatmospheric reentry vehicle interceptor subsystem
FABMDS	Field Army Ballistic Missile Defense System
FLAG	flexible, lightweight, agile guidance
GBR	ground-based radar
HEDI	high endoatmospheric defense interceptor
HIT	homing interceptor technology
HOE	Homing Overlay Experiment
IOC	initial operating capability
LED	low endoatmospheric defense
LEDI	low endoatmospheric defense interceptor
LWIR	long wavelength infrared
MAD	Mutual Assured Destruction
MICOM	Missile Command
QMR	qualitative materiel requirement
RPV	remotely piloted vehicle
SAM-D	surface-to-air missile—development
SDI	Strategic Defense Initiative
SES	shoot-evaluate-shoot
SRBM	short-range ballistic missile
SRS	Systems Requirement Study
SSTS	space surveillance and tracking system
SWIR	short wavelength infrared
TBM	tactical ballistic missile
TIR	thermal-imaging radar

PERGAMON-BRASSEY'S
International Defense Publishers

List of Publications
published for the
Institute for Foreign Policy Analysis, Inc.

Orders for the following titles should be addressed to: Pergamon-Brassey's, Maxwell House, Fairview Park, Elmsford, New York, 10523; or to Pergamon-Brassey's, Headington Hill Hall, Oxford, OX3 0BW, England.

Foreign Policy Reports

ETHICS, DETERRENCE, AND NATIONAL SECURITY. By James E. Dougherty, Midge Decter, Pierre Hassner, Laurence Martin, Michael Novak, and Vladimir Bukovsky. 1985. xvi, 91pp. $9.95.

AMERICAN SEA POWER AND GLOBAL STRATEGY. By Robert J. Hanks. 1985. viii, 92pp. $9.95.

DECISION-MAKING IN COMMUNIST COUNTRIES: AN INSIDE VIEW. By Jan Sejna and Joseph D. Douglass, Jr. 1986. xii, 75pp. $9.95.

NATIONAL SECURITY: ETHICS, STRATEGY, AND POLITICS. A LAYMAN'S PRIMER. By Robert L. Pfaltzgraff, Jr. 1986. v, 37pp. $9.95.

DETERRING CHEMICAL WARFARE: U.S. POLICY OPTIONS FOR THE 1990S. By Hugh Stringer. 1986. xii, 71pp. $9.95.

THE CRISIS OF COMMUNISM: ITS MEANING, ORIGINS, AND PHASES. By Rett R. Ludwikowski. 1986. xii, 79pp. $9.95.

THE REORGANIZATION OF THE JOINT CHIEFS OF STAFF: A CRITICAL ANALYSIS. Contributions by Allan R. Millett, Mackubin Thomas Owens, Bernard E. Trainor, Edward C. Meyer, and Robert Murray. 1986. xi, 67pp. $9.95.

Special Reports

STRATEGIC MINERALS AND INTERNATIONAL SECURITY. Edited by Uri Ra'anan and Charles M. Perry. 1985. viii, 85pp. $9.95.

THIRD WORLD MARXIST-LENINIST REGIMES: STRENGTHS, VULNERABILITIES, AND U.S. POLICY. By Uri Ra'anan, Francis Fukuyama, Mark Falcoff, Sam C. Sarkesian, and Richard H. Shultz, Jr. 1985. xv, 125pp. $9.95.

THE RED ARMY ON PAKISTAN'S BORDER: POLICY IMPLICATIONS FOR THE UNITED STATES. By Anthony Arnold, Richard P. Cronin, Thomas Perry Thornton, Theodore L. Eliot, Jr., and Robert L. Pfaltzgraff, Jr. 1986. vi, 83pp. $9.95.

ASYMMETRIES IN U.S. AND SOVIET STRATEGIC DEFENSE PROGRAMS: IMPLICATIONS FOR NEAR-TERM AMERICAN DEPLOYMENT OPTIONS. By William A. Davis, Jr. 1986. xi, 71pp. $9.95.

Books

ATLANTIC COMMUNITY IN CRISIS: A REDEFINITION OF THE ATLANTIC RELATIONSHIP. Edited by Walter F. Hahn and Robert L. Pfaltzgraff, Jr. 1979. 386pp. $43.00.

REVISING U.S. MILITARY STRATEGY: TAILORING MEANS TO ENDS. By Jeffrey Record. 1984. 113pp. $16.95 ($9.95, paper).

SHATTERING EUROPE'S DEFENSE CONSENSUS: THE ANTINUCLEAR PROTEST MOVEMENT AND THE FUTURE OF NATO. Edited by James E. Dougherty and Robert L. Pfaltzgraff, Jr. 1985. 226pp. $18.95.

INSTITUTE FOR FOREIGN POLICY ANALYSIS, INC.
List of Publications

Orders for the following titles in IFPA's series of Special Reports, Foreign Policy Reports, National Security Papers, Conference Reports, and Books should be addressed to the Circulation Manager, Institute for Foreign Policy Analysis, Central Plaza Building, Tenth Floor, 675 Massachusetts Avenue, Cambridge, Massachusetts 02139-3396. (Telephone: 617-492-2116.) Please send a check or money order for the correct amount together with your order.

Foreign Policy Reports

DEFENSE TECHNOLOGY AND THE ATLANTIC ALLIANCE: COMPETITION OR COLLABORATION? By Frank T.J. Bray and Michael Moodie. April 1977. vi, 42pp. $5.00.

IRAN'S QUEST FOR SECURITY: U.S. ARMS TRANSFERS AND THE NUCLEAR OPTION. By Alvin J. Cottrell and James E. Dougherty. May 1977. 59pp. $5.00.

ETHIOPIA, THE HORN OF AFRICA, AND U.S. POLICY. By John H. Spencer. September 1977. 69pp. $5.00.

BEYOND THE ARAB-ISRAELI SETTLEMENT: NEW DIRECTIONS FOR U.S. POLICY IN THE MIDDLE EAST. By R.K. Ramazani. September 1977. viii, 69pp. $5.00.

SPAIN, THE MONARCHY AND THE ATLANTIC COMMUNITY. By David C. Jordan. June 1979. v, 55pp. $5.00.

U.S. STRATEGY AT THE CROSSROADS: TWO VIEWS. By Robert J. Hanks and Jeffrey Record. July 1982. viii, 69pp. $7.50.

THE U.S. MILITARY PRESENCE IN THE MIDDLE EAST: PROBLEMS AND PROSPECTS. By Robert J. Hanks. December 1982. vii, 77pp. $7.50.

SOUTHERN AFRICA AND WESTERN SECURITY. By Robert J. Hanks. August 1983. vii, 71pp. $7.50.

THE WEST GERMAN PEACE MOVEMENT AND THE NATIONAL QUESTION. By Kim R. Holmes. March 1984. x, 73pp. $7.50.

THE HISTORY AND IMPACT OF MARXIST-LENINIST ORGANIZATIONAL THEORY. By John P. Roche. April 1984. x, 70pp. $7.50.

Special Reports

THE CRUISE MISSILE: BARGAINING CHIP OR DEFENSE BARGAIN? By Robert L. Pfaltzgraff, Jr., and Jacquelyn K. Davis. January 1977. x, 53pp. $3.00.

EUROCOMMUNISM AND THE ATLANTIC ALLIANCE. By James E. Dougherty and Diane K. Pfaltzgraff. January 1977. xiv, 66pp. $3.00.

THE NEUTRON BOMB: POLITICAL, TECHNICAL, AND MILITARY ISSUES. By S.T. Cohen. November 1978. xii, 95pp. $6.50.

SALT II AND U.S.-SOVIET STRATEGIC FORCES. By Jacquelyn K. Davis, Patrick J. Friel, and Robert L. Pfaltzgraff, Jr. June 1979. xii, 51pp. $5.00.

THE EMERGING STRATEGIC ENVIRONMENT: IMPLICATIONS FOR BALLISTIC MISSILE DEFENSE. By Leon Gouré, William G. Hyland, and Colin S. Gray. December 1979. xi, 75pp. $6.50.

THE SOVIET UNION AND BALLISTIC MISSILE DEFENSE. By Jacquelyn K. Davis, Uri Ra'anan, Robert L. Pfaltzgraff, Jr., Michael J. Deane, and John M. Collins. March 1980. xi, 71pp. $6.50. (Out of print).

ENERGY ISSUES AND ALLIANCE RELATIONSHIPS: THE UNITED STATES, WESTERN EUROPE AND JAPAN. By Robert L. Pfaltzgraff, Jr. April 1980. xii, 71pp. $6.50.

U.S. STRATEGIC-NUCLEAR POLICY AND BALLISTIC MISSILE DEFENSE: THE 1980S AND BEYOND. By William Schneider, Jr., Donald G. Brennan, William A. Davis, Jr., and Hans Rühle. April 1980. xii, 61pp. $6.50.

THE UNNOTICED CHALLENGE: SOVIET MARITIME STRATEGY AND THE GLOBAL CHOKE POINTS. By Robert J. Hanks. August 1980. xi, 66pp. $6.50.

FORCE REDUCTIONS IN EUROPE: STARTING OVER. By Jeffrey Record. October 1980. xi, 91pp. $6.50.

SALT II AND AMERICAN SECURITY. By Gordon J. Humphrey, William R. Van Cleave, Jeffrey Record, William H. Kincade, and Richard Perle. October 1980. xvi, 65pp.

THE FUTURE OF U.S. LAND-BASED STRATEGIC FORCES. By Jake Garn, J.I. Coffey, Lord Chalfont, and Ellery B. Block. December 1980. xvi, 80pp.

THE CAPE ROUTE: IMPERILED WESTERN LIFELINE. By Robert J. Hanks. February 1981. xi, 80pp. $6.50. (Hardcover, $10.00).

POWER PROJECTION AND THE LONG-RANGE COMBAT AIRCRAFT: MISSIONS, CAPABILITIES AND ALTERNATIVE DESIGNS. By Jacquelyn K. Davis and Robert L. Pfaltzgraff, Jr. June 1981. ix, 37pp. $6.50.

THE PACIFIC FAR EAST: ENDANGERED AMERICAN STRATEGIC POSITION. By Robert J. Hanks. October 1981. vii, 75pp. $7.50.

NATO'S THEATER NUCLEAR FORCE MODERNIZATION PROGRAM: THE REAL ISSUES. By Jeffrey Record. November 1981. viii, 102pp. $7.50.

THE CHEMISTRY OF DEFEAT: ASYMMETRIES IN U.S. AND SOVIET CHEMICAL WARFARE POSTURES. By Amoretta M. Hoeber. December 1981. xiii, 91pp. $6.50.

THE HORN OF AFRICA: A MAP OF POLITICAL-STRATEGIC CONFLICT. By James E. Dougherty. April 1982. xv, 74pp. $7.50.

THE WEST, JAPAN AND CAPE ROUTE IMPORTS: THE OIL AND NON-FUEL MINERAL TRADES. By Charles Perry. June 1982. xiv, 88pp. $7.50.

THE RAPID DEPLOYMENT FORCE AND U.S. MILITARY INTERVENTION IN THE PERSIAN GULF. By Jeffrey Record. May 1983, Second Edition. viii, 83pp. $7.50.

THE GREENS OF WEST GERMANY: ORIGINS, STRATEGIES, AND TRANSATLANTIC IMPLICATIONS. By Robert L. Pfaltzgraff, Jr., Kim R. Holmes, Clay Clemens, and Werner Kaltefleiter. August 1983. xi, 105pp. $7.50.

THE ATLANTIC ALLIANCE AND U.S. GLOBAL STRATEGY. By Jacquelyn K. Davis and Robert L. Pfaltzgraff, Jr. September 1983. x, 44pp. $7.50.

WORLD ENERGY SUPPLY AND INTERNATIONAL SECURITY. By Herman Franssen, John P. Hardt, Jacquelyn K. Davis, Robert J. Hanks, Charles Perry, Robert L. Pfaltzgraff, Jr., and Jeffrey Record. October 1983. xiv, 93pp. $7.50.

POISONING ARMS CONTROL: THE SOVIET UNION AND CHEMICAL/BIOLOGICAL WEAPONS. By Mark C. Storella. June 1984. xi, 99pp. $7.50.

National Security Papers

CBW: THE POOR MAN'S ATOMIC BOMB. By Neil C. Livingstone and Joseph D. Douglass, Jr., with a Foreword by Senator John Tower. February 1984. x, 33pp. $5.00.

U.S. STRATEGIC AIRLIFT: REQUIREMENTS AND CAPABILITIES. By Jeffrey Record. January 1986. vi, 38pp. $6.00.

STRATEGIC BOMBERS: HOW MANY ARE ENOUGH? By Jeffrey Record. January 1986. vi, 22pp. $6.00.

STRATEGIC DEFENSE AND EXTENDED DETERRENCE: A NEW TRANSATLANTIC DEBATE. By Jacquelyn K. Davis and Robert L. Pfaltzgraff, Jr. February 1986. viii, 51pp. $8.00.

JCS REORGANIZATION AND U.S. ARMS CONTROL POLICY. By James E. Dougherty. March 1986. xiv, 27pp. $6.00.

STRATEGIC FORCE MODERNIZATION AND ARMS CONTROL. Contributions by Edward L. Rowny, R. James Woolsey, Harold Brown, Alexander M. Haig, Jr., Albert Gore, Jr., Brent Scowcroft, Russell E. Dougherty, A. Casey, Gordon Fornell, and Sam Nunn. 1986. xiii, 43pp. $6.00.

U.S. BOMBER FORCE MODERNIZATION. Contributions by Mike Synar, Richard K. Betts, William Kaufmann, Russell E. Dougherty, Richard DeLauer, and Dan Quayle. 1986. vii, 9pp. $5.00.

U.S. STRATEGIC AIRLIFT CHOICES. Contributions by William S. Cohen, Russell Murray, Frederick G. Kroesen, William Kaufmann, Harold Brown, James A. Courter, and Robert W. Komer. 1986. ix, 13pp. $5.00.

Books

SOVIET MILITARY STRATEGY IN EUROPE. By Joseph D. Douglass, Jr. Pergamon Press, 1980. 252pp. (Out of print).

THE WARSAW PACT: ARMS, DOCTRINE, AND STRATEGY. By William J. Lewis. New York: McGraw-Hill Publishing Co., 1982. 471pp. $15.00.

THE BISHOPS AND NUCLEAR WEAPONS: THE CATHOLIC PASTORAL LETTER ON WAR AND PEACE. By James E. Dougherty. Archon Books, 1984. 255pp. $22.50.

Conference Reports

NATO AND ITS FUTURE: A GERMAN-AMERICAN ROUNDTABLE. Summary of a Dialogue. 1978. 22pp. $1.00.

SECOND GERMAN-AMERICAN ROUNDTABLE ON NATO: THE THEATER-NUCLEAR BALANCE. 1978. 32pp. $1.00.

THE SOVIET UNION AND BALLISTIC MISSILE DEFENSE. 1978. 26pp. $1.00.

U.S. STRATEGIC-NUCLEAR POLICY AND BALLISTIC MISSILE DEFENSE: THE 1980S AND BEYOND. 1979. 30pp. $1.00.

SALT II AND AMERICAN SECURITY. 1979. 39pp.

THE FUTURE OF U.S. LAND-BASED STRATEGIC FORCES. 1979. 32pp.

THE FUTURE OF NUCLEAR POWER. 1980. 48pp. $1.00.

THIRD GERMAN-AMERICAN ROUNDTABLE ON NATO: MUTUAL AND BALANCED FORCE REDUCTIONS IN EUROPE. 1980. 27pp. $1.00.

FOURTH GERMAN-AMERICAN ROUNDTABLE ON NATO: NATO MODERNIZATION AND EUROPEAN SECURITY. 1981. 15pp. $1.00.

SECOND ANGLO-AMERICAN SYMPOSIUM ON DETERRENCE AND EUROPEAN SECURITY. 1981. 25pp. $1.00.

THE U.S. DEFENSE MOBILIZATION INFRASTRUCTURE: PROBLEMS AND PRIORITIES. The Tenth Annual Conference, sponsored by the International Security Studies Program, The Fletcher School of Law and Diplomacy, Tufts University. 1981. 25pp. $1.00.

U.S. STRATEGIC DOCTRINE FOR THE 1980S. 1982. 14pp.

FRENCH-AMERICAN SYMPOSIUM ON STRATEGY, DETERRENCE AND EUROPEAN SECURITY. 1982. 14pp. $1.00.

FIFTH GERMAN-AMERICAN ROUNDTABLE ON NATO: THE CHANGING CONTEXT OF THE EUROPEAN SECURITY DEBATE. Summary of a Transatlantic Dialogue. 1982. 22pp. $1.00.

ENERGY SECURITY AND THE FUTURE OF NUCLEAR POWER. 1982. 39pp. $2.50.

INTERNATIONAL SECURITY DIMENSIONS OF SPACE. The Eleventh Annual Conference, sponsored by the International Security Studies Program, The Fletcher School of Law and Diplomacy, Tufts University. 1982. 24pp. $2.50.

PORTUGAL, SPAIN AND TRANSATLANTIC RELATIONS. Summary of a Transatlantic Dialogue. 1983. 18pp. $2.50.

JAPANESE-AMERICAN SYMPOSIUM ON REDUCING STRATEGIC MINERALS VULNERABILITIES: CURRENT PLANS, PRIORITIES, AND POSSIBILITIES FOR COOPERATION. 1983. 31pp. $2.50.

NATIONAL SECURITY POLICY: THE DECISION-MAKING PROCESS. The Twelfth Annual Conference, sponsored by the International Security Studies Program, The Fletcher School of Law and Diplomacy, Tufts University. 1983. 28pp. $2.50.

THE SECURITY OF THE ATLANTIC, IBERIAN AND NORTH AFRICAN REGIONS. Summary of a Transatlantic Dialogue. 1983. 25pp. $2.50.

THE WEST EUROPEAN ANTINUCLEAR PROTEST MOVEMENT: IMPLICATIONS FOR WESTERN SECURITY. Summary of a Transatlantic Dialogue. 1984. 21pp. $2.50.

THE U.S.-JAPANESE SECURITY RELATIONSHIP IN TRANSITION. Summary of a Transpacific Dialogue. 1984. 23pp. $2.50.

SIXTH GERMAN-AMERICAN ROUNDTABLE ON NATO: NATO AND EUROPEAN SECURITY—BEYOND INF. Summary of a Transatlantic Dialogue. 1984. 31pp. $2.50.

SECURITY COMMITMENTS AND CAPABILITIES: ELEMENTS OF AN AMERICAN GLOBAL STRATEGY. The Thirteenth Annual Conference, sponsored by the International Security Studies Program, The Fletcher School of Law and Diplomacy, Tufts University. 1984. 21pp. $2.50.

THIRD JAPANESE-AMERICAN-GERMAN CONFERENCE ON THE FUTURE OF NUCLEAR ENERGY. 1984. 40pp. $2.50.

SEVENTH GERMAN-AMERICAN ROUNDTABLE ON NATO: POLITICAL CONSTRAINTS, EMERGING TECHNOLOGIES, AND ALLIANCE STRATEGY. Summary of a Transatlantic Dialogue. 1985. 36pp. $2.50.

TERRORISM AND OTHER "LOW-INTENSITY" OPERATIONS: INTERNATIONAL LINKAGES. The Fourteenth Annual Conference, sponsored by the International Security Studies Program, The Fletcher School of Law and Diplomacy, Tufts University. 1985. 21pp. $2.50.

EAST-WEST TRADE AND TECHNOLOGY TRANSFER: NEW CHALLENGES FOR THE UNITED STATES. Second Annual Forum, co-sponsored by the Institute for Foreign Policy Analysis and the International Security Studies Program, The Fletcher School of Law and Diplomacy, Tufts University. 1986. 40pp. $3.50.

ORGANIZING FOR NATIONAL SECURITY: THE ROLE OF THE JOINT CHIEFS OF STAFF. 1986. 32pp. $2.50.

EIGHTH GERMAN-AMERICAN ROUNDTABLE ON NATO: STRATEGIC DEFENSE, NATO MODERNIZATION, AND EAST-WEST RELATIONS. Summary of a Transatlantic Dialogue. 1986. 47pp. $2.50.

EMERGING DOCTRINES AND TECHNOLOGIES: IMPLICATIONS FOR GLOBAL AND REGIONAL POLITICAL-MILITARY BALANCES. The Fifteenth Annual Conference, sponsored by the International Security Studies Program, The Fletcher School of Law and Diplomacy, Tufts University. 1986. 49pp. $2.50.

STRATEGIC WAR TERMINATION: POLITICAL-MILITARY-DIPLOMATIC DIMENSIONS. 1986. 22pp. $2.50.

Regional Security and Anti-Tactical Ballistic Missiles: Political and Technical Issues

This study assesses the political and technical dimensions of anti-tactical ballistic missile (ATBM) development in the United States since the early 1950s. Special attention is given to the obstacles which impeded the ATBM program, notably the perception that tactical missiles would never become a serious threat to the field army; that technology could not provide a truly effective countermeasure; that ATBM is destabilizing in the context of the INF balance in Western Europe; that defensive measures have a negative impact on extended deterrence and flexible response; and that ambiguities exist regarding whether an ATBM system is permitted under the ABM Treaty. The author examines Soviet ATBM developments and the Soviet tactical missile threat, and then assesses viable U.S. ATBM options in the near term, including nonnuclear air defense spinoffs from the current U.S. SDI program. He argues that the United States should embark on an ATBM prototype hardware development program since the essential outlines of the systems needed are discernible, the technology is within grasp, and the urgency of the Soviet threat makes further delay extremely risky.

William A. Davis, Jr., was formerly the Deputy Program Manager of the Army's ballistic missile defense (BMD) program. Prior to that, he served for five years as Director of the BMD Advanced Technology Program, and devoted a total of thirteen years to the BMD program. Following retirement from the government in 1982, he worked for three years as Vice President, Space Defense, at Teledyne Brown Engineering. During his government career, Davis was a major contributor to national studies of the defense of Minuteman and other military targets; and he played a prominent role in BMD experiments such as the Homing Overlay Experiment (HOE), which resulted in the first successful nonnuclear intercept of an ICBM target. He is the recipient of the Presidential Meritorious Executive Award and the Department of the Army Decoration for Exceptional Civilian Service. He is the author of *Asymmetries in U.S. and Soviet Strategic Defense Programs: Implications for Near-Term American Deployment Options* (published in 1986 by the Institute for Foreign Policy Analysis).

"Bill Davis makes a compelling case for immediate development of an integrated prototype anti-tactical ballistic missile system, as a response to Soviet capabilities which have created serious strategic and tactical imbalances. He defines an ABM treaty compliant prototype system that would contribute significantly to allied and theater defense, and also serve as a rapidly deployable lower tier SDI hedge option for CONUS defense."

Brig. General John G. Jones,
U.S. Army (Retired)
Commander of the U.S. Army Ballistic
Missile Defense Systems Command,
1975–1977

Design: William B. Bird

ISBN 0-08-035175-1